Essential
Costa
Brava

by Tony Kelly

Tony Kelly took up travel writing after
teaching English in Sudan and China. He
writes regularly for newspapers and
magazines, specialising in walking and the
outdoors. When not travelling he lives on a
farm in eastern England with his wife and
young son. He has also written *AA Essential*
guides to Menorca and Mallorca.

*Above: fishing boats in the sheltered harbour
at Arenys de Mar*

AA Publishing

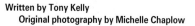

Written by Tony Kelly
Original photography by Michelle Chaplow

Published and distributed in the United
Kingdom by AA Publishing, a trading name
of Automobile Association Developments
Limited, whose registered office is Norfolk
House, Priestley Road, Basingstoke,
Hampshire, RG24 9NY.
Registered number 1878835.

Above: *walking in the
Garrotxa Natural Park*

Front cover: *Flamenco
dancer; Tossa de Mar;
wine marque*
Back cover: *olives*

A CIP catalogue record for this book is available from the
British Library.

ISBN 0 7495 1907 X

The contents of this publication are believed correct at
the time of printing. Nevertheless, the publishers cannot
be held responsible for any errors or omissions or for
changes in the details given in this guide or for the
consequences of any reliance on the information it
provides. Assessments of attractions, hotels, restaurants
and other sights are based upon the author's personal
experience and, therefore, necessarily contain elements of
subjective opinion which may not reflect the publisher's
opinion or dictate a reader's own experience on another
occasion.

We have tried to ensure accuracy in this guide, but
things do change and we would be grateful if readers
would advise us of any inaccuracies they may encounter.

Find out more about
AA Publishing and the
wide range of services
the AA provides by
visiting our web site at
www.theAA.com

Colour separation: Pace Colour, Southampton
Printed and bound in Italy by Printer Trento S.r.l.

Contents

About this Book

KEY TO SYMBOLS

🕂 map reference to the maps found in the What to See section

✉ address or location

☎ telephone number

🕓 opening times

🍴 restaurant or café on premises or near by

🚇 nearest underground train station

🚌 nearest bus/tram route

🚊 nearest overground train station

🛳 ferry crossings and boat excursions

✈ travel by air

ℹ tourist information

♿ facilities for visitors with disabilities

✋ admission charge

↔ other places of interest near by

❓ other practical information

▶ indicates the page where you will find a fuller description

Essential *Costa Brava* is divided into five sections to cover the most important aspects of your visit to Costa Brava.

Viewing Costa Brava pages 5–14
An introduction to Costa Brava by the author.
Costa Brava's Features
Essence of Costa Brava
The Shaping of Costa Brava
Peace and Quiet
Costa Brava's Famous

Top Ten pages 15–26
The author's choice of the Top Ten places to see in Costa Brava, each with practical information.

What to See pages 27–90
The three main areas of Costa Brava, each with its own brief introduction and an alphabetical listing of the main attractions.
Practical information
Snippets of 'Did you know…' information
5 suggested walks
3 suggested drives
2 features

Where To… pages 91–116
Detailed listings of the best places to eat, stay, shop, take the children and be entertained.

4

Practical Matters pages 117–24
A highly visual section containing essential travel information.

Maps
All map references are to the individual maps found in the What to See section of this guide.
For example, Monestir de Vilabertran has the reference 🕂 29E4 – indicating the page on which the map is located and the grid square in which the 11th-century monastery is to be found. A list of the maps that have been used in this travel guide can be found in the index.

Prices
Where appropriate, an indication of the cost of an establishment is given by **£** signs:
£££ denotes higher prices, **££** denotes average prices, while **£** denotes lower charges.

Star Ratings
Most of the places described in this book have been given a separate rating:
✪✪✪ Do not miss
✪✪ Highly recommended
✪ Worth seeing

Viewing
Costa Brava

Above: *Cadaqués harbour*
Right: *traditional Catalan costume*

5

Tony Kelly's Costa Brava

What Does it Mean?

The word *bravo* or *brava* can have several, slightly different meanings. Referring to a landscape, it means 'wild and rugged'; applied to the sea, it means 'stormy' – like the Costa Brava when it is lashed by the *tramuntana* wind. People who are *bravo* are brave and spirited – perhaps a metaphor for the Catalan people and their long struggle for recognition.

The usually calm waters of the Costa Brava are perfect for boating and diving

Costa Brava – 'the Wild Coast'. The name was coined by a local journalist, Ferran Agulló, in 1908, gazing out at the rugged coastline of pine-clad cliffs and coves. At times you could be forgiven for thinking he was referring to the nightlife, rather than the scenery.

When tourists started visiting Spain in the 1950s, it was to the Costa Brava that they came. Other, bigger *costas* followed, but it was this small corner near the French border that led the way. Fishing villages were transformed almost overnight into high-rise resorts; the face of the coastline changed more in a generation than in the previous thousand years. The Costa Brava virtually invented the sun-and-sea holiday.

Yet those rocky creeks still exist. There are villas climbing up the hillsides now, but this is still recognisable as Agulló's Wild Coast. There are areas of unspoilt marshland, Greek and Roman ruins and long, sandy beaches with not a hotel in sight. The main town, Girona, has a charming, medieval heart, and further inland are solid Catalan towns like Olot and Vic. Catalunya (Catalonia) is enjoying a cultural renaissance, seen most visibly in the revival of the Catalan language and of the *sardana* dance. The red-and-gold Catalan flag flies above government buildings and the people look to Barcelona, rather than Madrid, as their capital. Like the new Catalonia, the Costa Brava is changing its image – no longer cheap and cheerful, but chic, confident and cool.

Costa Brava's Features

Geography and Climate
• The Costa Brava begins at Blanes, 60km north of Barcelona, and continues around the coast for 220km to the French border at Portbou.
• There are 119 official beaches, with a total length of 56km – a quarter of the entire coastline.
• The average summer temperature is 26°C, and there are more than 200 days of sunshine a year. The sea temperature reaches 24°C in August and is pleasantly warm from June to October. The *tramuntana*, a cold north wind, can strike at any time.

Language
Catalan (▶ 124) has been the official language of Catalonia since 1979, though Spanish is also widely spoken and understood. Most signs and menus are in Catalan, which is used throughout this book. English, French and German are all widely spoken in the coastal resorts.

Government and Economy
• The Costa Brava belongs to Girona province, itself part of Catalunya (Catalonia), a semi-autonomous region of Spain since 1979. Catalonia is the wealthiest region in Spain, producing 20 per cent of the country's gross national product.

People
• The population of the Costa Brava region rises from around 425,000 in winter to a million in summer. The capital, Girona, has a population of 75,000. Catalonia has the highest population density of any region in Spain.

Tourism
• More than 5 million foreign tourists visit the Costa Brava each year. In 1996, 44 per cent of visitors came from France, 12 per cent from Germany, 6 per cent from the Netherlands and 5 per cent from the United Kingdom.

• The Costa Brava is the favourite holiday destination among Catalans, who make two million visits to the area each year.
• In peak season the Costa Brava has more than 80,000 hotel beds, 100,000 places in campsites and 500,000 in self-catering villas and apartments.

The warm summer climate means that life is lived out of doors

7

Essence of the Costa Brava

You cannot separate the Costa Brava from Catalonia. History has given the Catalans a fiercely independent spirit, looking outwards, to Europe, as much as in, to the Iberian peninsula. The first Greek and Roman settlers landed here; French art and architecture crossed into Spain over the Pyrenees. It is no surprise that this is where Spain's large-scale tourist began. The Catalans are courteous, businesslike, conservative and welcoming, but with little of the flamboyance of their Spanish neighbours. In the expected Mediterranean way, they know how to take life slowly – but they also know how to get things done.

Ancient and modern exist side by side, as at Tossa de Mar (below)

THE **10** ESSENTIALS

*If you only have a short time to visit the Costa
Brava, or would like to get a really complete
picture of the region, here are the essentials:*

Left: *Lloret de Mar; lie
back and soak up the sun
in Costa Brava style*

Above: *the markets sell
fresh produce and
speciality sausages*

Below: *colours blaze in
locally made pottery*

• **Follow the winding coast
road** from Tossa to Sant
Feliu (➤ 81), then explore
the rocky coves around
Begur and Palafrugell that
gave the Costa Brava its
name.

• **Go diving or snorkelling**
in the clear waters around
the Medes islands (➤ 45),
whose reefs and caves
harbour an abundance of
underwater life.

• **Visit the fish markets** in
Blanes, Palamós and Roses
(➤ 106), then dine out-of-
doors on some of the
freshest seafood you will
ever eat.

• **Relax in the botanical
gardens** at Cap Roig and
Blanes (➤ 43, 76), where
Mediterranean plants grow
on cliffsides overlooking the
sea.

• **Wander the back streets
of Girona**, with its carefully

restored Jewish quarter and
medieval mansions
(➤ 31–9).

• **Visit the surreal Dalí
museum** in Figueres
(➤ 25), then follow the
Salvador Dalí trail from
Portlligat to Puból (➤ 69).

• **Head for one of the inland
towns on market day**
(➤ 106) for a real taste of
Catalan life. One of the best
is the Saturday market at Vic
(➤ 86).

• **Browse in the pottery
shops** of La Bisbal (➤ 42,
108) and take home a
souvenir of your visit.

• **Take a boat trip** along
the coast around the wild
northern coastline between
Roses and Cap de Creus.

• **Lie on the beach** soaking
up the sun – the authentic
Costa Brava experience.
But don't forget your
sunblock!

9

The Shaping of the Costa Brava

By the 7th century BC
Iberian settlers, probably from northern Africa, establish the first towns at Ullastret and elsewhere.

By 550 BC
The Greeks establish trading posts at Empúries and Roses.

218 BC
The Romans land at Empúries to begin their conquest of the Iberian peninsula. Olives and vines are introduced; Catalan develops as a vernacular form of Latin.

5th century AD
Roman rule collapses and the region is occupied by Visigoths, who name it Gotalonia.

717
Muslim occupation of Catalonia. Unlike elsewhere in Spain, this lasts less than 100 years. Girona is captured by Charlemagne in 785.

878
Wilfred the Hairy becomes the first Count of Barcelona, ruling over an area roughly equivalent to modern Catalonia. Following his death in 897, his dynasty rules for 500 years.

The Catalan flag

1137
Catalonia and Aragón are united. The new kingdom becomes a major Mediterranean power, with an empire extending to Sicily, Sardinia, Malta and the Balearics. Catalan becomes the official language and the first Catalan literature is published. The *Corts Catalans*, with representatives from the people, the clergy and the nobility, are the first form of parliamentary government in Europe.

1469
Fernando of Aragón marries Isabella of Castile. Following the final defeat of the Moors, Aragón and Castile unite with Granada in 1492 to create modern Spain. Jews are expelled from Girona and elsewhere.

1640
The revolt of *Els Segadors* (the harvesters)

Catalonia was active in the fight against Fascism during the Spanish Civil War

against Spanish rule during the Thirty Years' War with France. Catalonia declares independence and places itself under the protection of the French king, finally surrendering to Spain in 1652.

1713
The Bourbon dynasty accedes to the throne following the War of the Spanish Succession. Felipe V bans the Catalan language and closes Catalonia's universities in retaliation for Catalonia supporting the Habsburg claims.

1808–14
Napoleon's troops occupy Catalonia. Girona is besieged for seven months in 1809.

19th century
Catalonia's industrial revolution makes it the wealthiest region in Spain. The cork and wine industries flourish, and Spain's first railway opens from Barcelona. Catalan nationalism is revived and there is an artistic and literary renaissance, seen in the *Modernista* architectural movement.

1924
Opening of the Hostal de la Gavina at S'Agaró.

1936–9
The Spanish Civil War. Catalonia is the final Republican stronghold, but surrenders in 1939.

1939–75
Dictatorship under General Franco. The Catalan language is banned, along with traditional festivals and the *sardana* dance.

1960s
The start of the tourist boom. Girona airport is opened and new resorts are developed at Lloret de Mar and Platja d'Aro.

Tossa de Mar, seen here in the 1960s, was one of the earliest tourist resorts

1975
Death of Franco. Juan Carlos becomes King of Spain.

1978
A new democratic constitution grants limited autonomy to the Spanish regions.

1979
Catalonia becomes an autonomous region, with Jordi Pujol as its president. Catalan is reinstated as the official language.

1983
Creation of the Aiguamolls de l'Empordà nature reserve.

1985
The Medes islands become Spain's first maritime nature reserve.

1986
Spain joins the European Community.

1992
The Olympic Games are held in Barcelona.

1996
After 14 years of socialist government, Spain elects a centre-right coalition, including Jordi Pujol's Catalan nationalist party.

King Juan Carlos

11

Peace & Quiet

Even in the height of summer it is easy to get away from it all on the Costa Brava. There may not be room to move on the beaches, but set back from the coastline is a region of cork and oak forests, waiting to be explored. Some tourist offices issue local walking maps, and some organise guided walks in summer. The GR92 long-distance coastal footpath runs through the region, waymarked with red-and-white stripes; shorter circular routes are marked in yellow and white.

For real peace and quiet, go out of season. The mild days of February, March, October and November can be perfect for walking, or even a sunny picnic on the beach. The quieter resorts have all closed down and you can have their pine-fringed coves to yourself, while towns like Blanes and Palamós have reverted to their original function as fishing ports.

Natural Parks

Growing environmental awareness since the return of democracy has led to the creation of several natural parks in the region, where wildlife is protected and development carefully controlled. There are two parks on the coast – at Aiguamolls de l'Empordà (► 23) and at Cap de Creus (► 64) – as well as the offshore marine reserve around the Medes islands (► 45). There are also three natural parks in the inland mountains, at Serra de l'Albera (► 71), Serra de Montseny (► 85) and the Garrotxa volcanic zone around Olot (► 47, 49). All have information centres and networks of well-marked walking trails. It is essential to keep to the paths and to avoid disturbing plants and wildlife.

Above: *wild flowers grow on the Pyrenean grasslands*

Below: *the garganey builds its nests among the Empordà marshes*

Fauna and Flora

The coastal region is an important breeding ground for wetland birds, especially in the Empordà marshes. Species which breed here throughout the year include purple herons, Kentish plovers, bee-eaters, marsh harriers and black-winged stilts. Flamingos, grey herons and white storks arrive during the spring and autumn migrating seasons, and in winter the lagoons are home to thousands of ducks. This is Spain's only breeding ground for the

garganey, a small brown teal with blue wing panels and a distinctive striped head. Seabirds such as razorbills, gannets, storm petrels and Cory's shearwaters are attracted to the Medes islands, which also support an important colony of herring gulls.

On walks in the inland forests you may encounter a red squirrel; other mammals include badgers, foxes and wild boar. Look out too for swallowtail butterflies, with their distinctive forked tails.

The coastal cliffs and the Pyrenean grasslands are studded with wild flowers in spring and early summer, including asphodels, gladioli, orchids and hyacinths. Thrift and milk-vetch grow on the cliffs at Cap de Creus, where the headland is carpeted with rosemary, lavender and Spanish broom. The mountains of the Serra de Montseny are the last remaining habitat of the white-flowered saxifrage. The botanical gardens at Blanes (➤ 76) and Calella de Palafrugell (➤ 43) have impressive collections of Mediterranean flowers, plants and trees.

Above: *the cork forests are a reminder of Catalonia's once-thriving cork industry*

Below: *the Empordàn plain stretches inland from the coast towards the Pyrenees*

Costa Brava's Famous

Dalí in Portlligat, where he spent more than 30 years

Salvador Dalí

The leading figure in the surrealist movement was born in Figueres in 1904 and had his first exhibition in 1919 in the theatre that was to become his memorial (➤ 25). After spells in New York and Paris, he returned to Catalonia and settled in Portlligat (➤ 68) with his lover Gala, whom he married in a secret ceremony in 1958. Unlike other artists, Dalí refused to go into exile during the Franco years, and in 1975 he sent the dying dictator a telegram of congratulations on the execution of five prisoners. In 1982 King Juan Carlos awarded Dalí the title of Marquis of Dalí of Púbol; Dalí responded by leaving all of his works to the Spanish state. Following Gala's death, Dalí moved into her castle at Púbol (➤ 18), but after setting fire to himself there in 1984 he lived out his remaining years in Figueres, dying in 1989 and being buried in the crypt of his museum. Dalí was a film-maker, novelist and fashion designer, but he is best known as the creator of the soft watch, a recurring theme from his paintings – and for the sexual obsessions which led him to recruit young models to make love while he watched.

FC Barcelona
FC Barcelona is a symbol of Catalan pride and success. The top Spanish team of recent years, Barcelona were European champions in 1992. Numerous foreign stars, including Diego Maradona, Johann Cruyff, Gary Lineker and Ronaldo, have been attracted to play at the Camp Nou, but the Catalan folk hero remains Ricardo Zamorra, the 'Cat', a star of the 1930s and the greatest Spanish goalkeeper of all time.

Jordi Pujol

In 1960 a young doctor was imprisoned for organising the singing of Catalan nationalist songs during a visit by General Franco to Barcelona. Twenty years later that same man was elected President of Catalonia. The leader of the conservative Convergència i Unió party has held the position ever since and has also become a force in national politics, using his party's votes to extract concessions for Catalonia from governments of both left and right.

Right: Jordi Pujol alongside Diana, Princess of Wales, in Girona, 1988

Top Ten

Above: *the curving bays of Tossa de Mar*
Right: *fisherman in Cadaqués*

1
Besalú

✝ 29D4

🍴 Choice of restaurants and cafés (£–££)

🚌 Buses from Figueres, Girona and Olot

ℹ️ Plaça Llibertat 1
☎ 972 59 12 40

↔️ Castellfollit de la Roca
(► 44)

❓ Market on Tue; Festa dels Dolors, evening procession on the Fri before Palm Sunday; *sardana* dancing on Easter Sunday; Festa Major, last weekend in Sep

A well–preserved medieval town centre at the heart of the region, with several Romanesque churches and the only Jewish bath house in Spain.

This small town at the confluence of the Fluvià and Capellada rivers was the historic capital of the Garrotxa region, ruled for more than 200 years by a dynasty established by Wilfred the Hairy. After the 12th century its importance declined, but following its declaration as a National Historic Monument in 1966 it has been restored to its former glory.

Come here on a Tuesday morning, when the porticoed central square, Plaça Llibertat, is buzzing with chatter and the market stalls are piled high with flowers, fruit and cheese, and you realise that this is still very much a working town. Along the cobbled streets which fan out from the square are delicatessens and antique shops, set among medieval arches, columns and Gothic windows. Of several Romanesque churches, the most impressive is the monastery church of Sant Pere, with a pair of stone lions adorning its façade.

The symbol of Besalú is its angled bridge over the Fluvià, built in the 11th century and destroyed several times, most recently in the Spanish Civil War. Arriving by car, park on the Banyoles side and enter Besalú across the bridge. Near here is the Mikwà, the only remains of a once significant Jewish community. This ritual bath house, with thermal springs and running water from the river, was used by men before prayer and by women before marriage, childbirth and menstruation. The tourist office will lend you the key for a modest charge.

In earlier times visitors paid a toll to enter Besalú across its medieval bridge

2
Cadaqués

This fishing village and stylish resort has long attracted a curious mixture of artists, tourists and people seeking an alternative way of life.

Brightly coloured fishing boats are moored in the bay

✚ 29F4

🍴 Wide choice of restaurants and bars (£–££)

🚌 Buses from Figueres and Roses

ℹ️ Carrer Cotxe 2 A
☎ 972 25 83 15

↔️ Cap de Creus (➤ 64), Portlligat (➤ 68)

❓ Market on Mon; Mare de Déu del Carme, procession of fishing boats on 16 Jul; international music and arts festival, Jul and Aug

Museu de Cadaqués

✉️ Carrer Narcís Monturiol 15

☎ 972 25 88 77

🕐 Hours vary according to exhibition. Usually, summer 10:30–1:30, 4–8; winter 4–8

✋ Moderate

Cadaqués appears at first sight to be a typical Mediterranean fishing village. It still is a fishing village, but it is much more than that. Picasso spent some time here in the early 20th century, but it was Salvador Dalí who really put Cadaqués on the map. His father came from here; it was here that he met his wife; and it was near here, at Portlligat, that he eventually settled down, attracted by the light, the remoteness and the rugged beauty of Spain's most easterly village.

There are reminders of Dalí everywhere: a statue on the seafront, a sundial on the façade of a hotel, the logo of the L'Hostal bar. In the 1960s, when hippies and intellectuals flocked to Dalí's side, Cadaqués was known as Spain's St Tropez. The same people still come to Cadaqués today.

There are several art galleries and stylish boutiques. The **Museo de Cadaqués** features contemporary Catalan artists as well as engravings by Dalí. The old town of steep and narrow streets winds its way up to the church of Santa Maria, with its baroque reredos.

3
Castell Gala Dalí, Púbol

 29E3

 972 67 75 00

 15 Mar–1 Nov, Tue–Sun
10:30–815; 15 Jun–15
Sep, daily 10:30–8

Can Bosch (£) near by,
in the village

Buses between Girona
and Palafrugell pass
about 2km away

Separate wheelchair
entrance

Moderate

*The castle which Salvador Dalí bought as a refuge
for his wife has become a homage to her memory
and to the couple's bizarre relationship.*

When Salvador and Gala Dalí were in exile in Italy during
the Spanish Civil War, the painter promised his wife that
he would one day buy her a castle. Thirty years later, he
acquired this Gothic and Renaissance castle in the village
of Púbol. Dalí wanted Gala to be able to get away from
him, with her lovers if necessary, and insisted that he
would never enter the castle without her permission.

The castle was in a state of disrepair and Dalí set about
re-creating it. The result is a typically Dalíesque mixture of
the grotesque, the beautiful and the absurd. Classical
statues in the garden share space with elephant figures

Above: *Dalí's Cadillac
must have looked out of
place in the small village
of Púbol (inset)*

sculpted from cement; 17th-century tapestries hang
beside *trompe l'oeil* painted radiators and huge Dalí
canvases. Everywhere you look there are portraits of Gala,
and her initial G is frequently worked into the design.

Gala spent little time in her castle, arriving for short
stays each summer but continuing to live with Dalí in
Portlligat. When she died in 1982 her body was driven to
Púbol and buried in the crypt – with a stuffed giraffe
looking on. Dalí moved into her room but two years later
he set fire to the bed and, despite a life-saving operation,
he was never to return to the castle. The Cadillac in which
he insisted on leaving Púbol – he refused to take an
ambulance – still sits in the garage. Dalí left the castle to
the Spanish state and it was opened to the public as a
museum in 1996.

4
Empúries

An ancient Greek and Roman settlement on the shores of the Gulf of Roses, where Spain first came into contact with wider European culture.

It was the Greeks who first established a trading post (*emporion*) here on what was then an island; contact between Greek settlers and indigenous tribes led to the development of the Iberian culture. The Romans anchored at Empúries in 218 BC, the first step on the route to the colonisation of Spain. The Roman city of Emporiae was abandoned in the 3rd century AD and only rediscovered by archaeologists in 1908. Much of it has still to be excavated.

The remains of the Roman city show how much Spanish town planning owes to Roman influence. The forum at the centre, the forerunner of the Plaça Major, would once have been surrounded by arcades; there were temples at one end and a main street leading to the city walls. Even the amphitheatre outside the walls has its equivalent in today's bullring or football stadium.

Below is the Greek city, dominated by a statue of Asklepios, the god of healing (the original is in Barcelona's archaeological museum). A small museum interprets the ruins, and there is an excellent audio-visual show. Afterwards you can walk along the seafront, past the original Greek jetty, to the village of Sant Martí d'Empúries, site of the first Greek settlement.

✚ 29E3

✉ 1km north of L'Escala

☎ 972 77 02 08

🕐 Jun–Sep, daily 10–8; Oct–May, daily 10–6. Closed 1 Jan, 25 Dec

🍴 Snack bar (£) on site, restaurants (£–££) in Sant Martí d'Empúries

🚌 Buses to L'Escala from Figueres, Girona and Palafrugell

♿ None

✋ Moderate; extra charge for audio-visual show

↔ L'Escala (► 66)

The Roman city contains some remarkably well-preserved mosaic floors

5
Girona Old Town

✚ 29D3

🍴 Choice of restaurants and cafés (£–£££)

🚌 Girona bus station, 1km away

🚉 Girona, 1km away

ℹ️ Rambla de la Llibertat 1
☎ 972 22 65 75

↔️ Girona (➤ 31–9)

❓ Holy Week procession on Good Friday

The restoration of the old quarter at the heart of Girona has been one of the great success stories of modern Catalonia.

As recently as 1964 the British travel writer Jan Morris described Girona as 'a shabby city of the north', but nobody could say that today. The political and cultural renaissance since 1980 has been accompanied by an architectural revival and a determination to show this historic city at its best. Dilapidated convents have been given new life as museums and art galleries; the university has been restored to its 16th-century home, and the narrow streets of the medieval Jewish district, the Call Jueu (➤ 32), have been carefully restored.

Above: the houses which back on to the River Onyar are the best-known image of Girona

This is a city for strolling, wandering at random among the maze of streets and going wherever a hidden archway or flight of steps leads you. Sun and shade, iron and stone, courtyards and balconies, narrow alleys and wide open squares, all come together here in perfect harmony.

Girona is at its most atmospheric in the streets of the old guilds. Between Plaça de l'Oli and Plaça del Vi, once the oil and wine markets, lies a network of narrow lanes, each named after a medieval trade. Carrer de l'Argenteria was once lined with silversmiths, Carrer de Mercaders with merchants, Carrer de les Ferreries Velles with blacksmiths and Carrer Peixateries Velles with fish-mongers. Their place have been taken by trendy cafés and boutiques, but the streets are still appealing.

Opposite: the medieval Jewish district is a maze of steep, cobbled streets

6
Monestir de Sant Pere de Rodes

 29E5

972 38 75 59

Jul–Sep, Tue–Sun 10–7;
Oct–May, Tue–Sun
10–5

None

El Port de la Selva (5km)

Vilajuïga (8km)

None

Moderate (free on Tue)

El Port de la Selva
(➤ 67)

Below: the road to the monastery (bottom) winds its way up a steep moutainside

This former Benedictine monastery in the hills above Cap de Creus has long been a place of pilgrimage, as much for its views as anything else.

Some claim that the monastery was built on the site of a Roman temple, but the more colourful story concerns Pope Boniface IV (608–615) and St Peter's head. With Rome under threat, the Pope ordered the church's most sacred relics to be sent to Spain for safe-keeping. When the time came to retrieve them, the head was nowhere to be found, so a monastery was built on the site here and dedicated to the saint. There are records of a monastery here from AD 878 – though recent excavations suggest that the site was in use long before that. The present church, dating from 1022, marks the transition to Romanesque architecture in Catalonia. The original cloister, its galleries decorated with murals, is covered by an upper cloister on the same level as the church. This was an important place of pilgrimage throughout the Middle Ages, but fell into decline after the 14th century. The last monks left in 1798.

There are good views of the monastery from the chapel of Santa Elena, all that remains of the village which grew up around the church. For the best views, climb the path behind the monastery to the ruined castle of Sant Salvador. Look down over the monastery and out to sea, then turn to see the Pyrenees on the horizon. The sunrises up here – some of the first in Spain – are magical.

7

Parc Natural de l'Aiguamolls de l'Empordà

This wetland nature reserve provides a refuge for wildlife and migrant birds and a peaceful haven for visitors escaping from the crowded beaches.

Well-marked trails let you explore the lagoons and marshes on foot

Once upon a time, marshes covered the coastal plain; Empúries (▶ 19) was an island and the Montgrí mountains were surrounded by fens. As the population grew, the marshes disappeared, at first as a result of agriculture and lately because of tourism. The building of the marina on former marshland at Empúria-brava (▶ 65), galvanised environmentalists into action, leading to the creation of this natural park in 1983.

Carp, mullet and eel thrive in the lakes; there are badgers, newts and voles, and otters are being reintroduced. Above all the Empordà marshes are an important refuge for aquatic and migrant birds. Herons, ducks and geese live on the ponds; other species that breed here include the stone-curlew and the black-winged stilt. This is Spain's only nesting ground for the garganey, a rare species of duck. Seabirds flock here in winter, and during the main migrant seasons (Mar to May and Aug to Oct), it is possible to see 100 species in a day.

At the information centre in **El Cortalet** you can pick up leaflets and maps, and hire out binoculars, field guides and wheelchairs. There are two easy, waymarked trails from here, each with hides overlooking the lagoons; in summer they can be combined with a walk along the beach in a two-hour circular trail.

✚ 29E4

El Cortalet

✉ Off the road from Castelló d'Empúries to Sant Pere Pescador

☎ 972 45 42 22

🕐 Trails open at all times

ℹ Information centre: Apr–Sep, 9:30–2, 4:30–7; Oct–Mar, 9:30–2, 3:30–6. Closed 1 Jan, 25 Dec

🍴 (££)

🚌 Castelló d'Empúries

♿ Good

✋ Free (charge for car parking)

❓ Keep to the paths at all times; be prepared for flooding in winter

8

Roses

The beach at Roses sits in a calm, sheltered bay

A fishing port and ancient Greek colony, Roses has become the tourist capital of the northern Costa Brava.

 29F4

 Wide choice of restaurants and cafés (£–£££)

 From Cadaqués and Figueres

Boat trips to Cadaqués and Cala Montjoi in summer

Avinguda de Rhode 101 ☎ 972 25 73 31

 Cadaqués (► 17), Castelló d'Empúries (► 65)

Market on Sun; Mare del Déu del Carme, procession of fishing boats on 16 Jul

Ciutadella de Roses

 Daily 9–7 in summer, 9–6 in winter

 Free

With 4km of sandy beach at the head of a great sweeping bay, Roses is the perfect setting for a bucket-and-spade holiday. The sheltered waters are ideal for watersports, with windsurfing, sailing and waterskiing all available. There are also several smaller coves, beginning with Canyelles and Almadrava, 3km beyond the fishing harbour to the southeast. A hair-raising drive across a rugged landscape leads to the remote creek of Cala Montjoi; on the way you pass the Creu d'en Cobertella, the largest prehistoric burial chamber in Catalonia, dating from 3000 BC.

Roses was founded in the 8th century BC by Greek settlers, who named it Rhodes after their homeland, but it was the Romans who developed the fishing industry which led to the town's wealth. It is still an important fishing port, with a population of 12,000, which rises to 80,000 in summer. With 50 hotels, five campsites and dozens of restaurants and bars, it is a little too lively for some; but if you want a traditional beach holiday, with easy access to the quieter north coast, this is the best place.

The star-shaped citadel (**Ciutadella**) at the entrance to town is a 16th-century fortress on the site of the original Greek city, with Roman and medieval remains within its walls – you can clamber over the ruins and look down into the moat. Another ruined castle, east of town, stands on the slopes of Puig Rom hill. Climb this hill at sunset for romantic views over the Bay of Roses with the snow-capped Pyrenees in the distance.

9
Teatre-Museu Dalí

The memorial which Salvador Dalí created for himself in his home town of Figueres is a journey through the imagination of a tortured genius.

After the Prado in Madrid, this is the most visited museum in Spain – but is it really a museum at all? Dalí, its creator, denied that it was, calling it 'a gigantic surrealist object'. Even the name theatre-museum has two meanings. It is built on the ruins of an old theatre, where Dalí had his first exhibition at the age of 14; but it is also a theatre because of the way we are meant to respond. Dalí did not want captions, or a catalogue; he wanted the 'audience' to be free to create their own surrealist experience.

From outside the view is dominated by the transparent dome on the roof, together with Dalí's trademark eggs on the façade. Once inside, you are drawn to the courtyard, with its central sculpture, *Rainy Taxi*, featuring a giant model of Dalí's wife Gala standing on a black Cadillac, with a tower of tractor tyres topped by a fishing boat. There are things you cannot miss – like the Mae West room, where a sofa and two fireplaces are turned by means of a lens into a pouting face. Sooner or later you reach the crypt, where Dalí is buried. He spent his last years here, in the Torre Galatea, and on his deathbed told the Mayor of Figueres he wanted to be buried in his theatre, rather than with Gala in her castle at Púbol.

✚ 29E4

✉ Plaça Gala-Salvador Dalí, Figueres

☎ 972 67 75 00

🕐 Jul–Sep, daily 9–8; Oct–Jun, Tue–Sun 10:30–6

🍴 (£–££)

🚌 Figueres bus station, 1km away

🚉 Figueres, 1km away

♿ Few   ✋ Moderate

❓ Night-time opening in Aug, 10–12:30
✋ Expensive

Below: *Dalí enjoyed playing tricks on his visitors – is that Abraham Lincoln (left), or is it a portrait of his wife?*

10
Tossa de Mar

✚ 29E1

🍴 Choice of restaurants and cafés (£–££)

🚌 From Lloret de Mar (and from Girona in summer)

⛴ Boats to other south coast resorts in summer

*Tossa de Mar –
a charming town in a
beautiful setting*

*The remains of a fortified medieval village look
down on a horseshoe beach, making Tossa the most
attractive of the Costa Brava resorts.*

One resort on the crowded southern coast stands out
head and shoulders above its neighbours. The beach alone
would be enough to draw visitors, with safe swimming
and sheltered sunbathing in an idyllic bay, and several
smaller coves within easy reach. But what makes Tossa
special is its walled medieval village (Vila Vella), standing
proudly above the bay as it has done for more than
800 years.

ℹ Avinguda del Pelegrí 25
☎ 972 34 01 08

↔ Lloret de Mar (▶ 80)

❓ Market Thu; pilgrimage
on foot to Santa Coloma
de Farners, 20 Jan; fast
painting contest, last
Sun in Aug

Climb from the main beach, Platja Gran, pausing to glance
back at the sea through the arched window of an
abandoned church, and you soon reach this attractive
village. It was established in 1186 by the Abbot of Ripoll on
the promontory of Mont Guardí. Beneath here, just behind
the beach, is the Vila Nova (New Town), a warren of back
streets and 19th-century houses around the parish church.

Tossa was one of the first places on the Costa Brava to
attract foreigners. The painter Marc Chagall spent the
summer of 1934 here and called it his 'blue paradise'. The
Museu Municipal, in the former Abbot's palace, contains
letters from Chagall, delighted that the museum was to
display one of his paintings. During Tossa's fast painting
competition each August, up to 200 artists attempt to
capture the atmosphere of the Vila Vella in a day.

What to See

Above: *clear skies and
deep blue seas*
Right: *flamenco dancers*

27

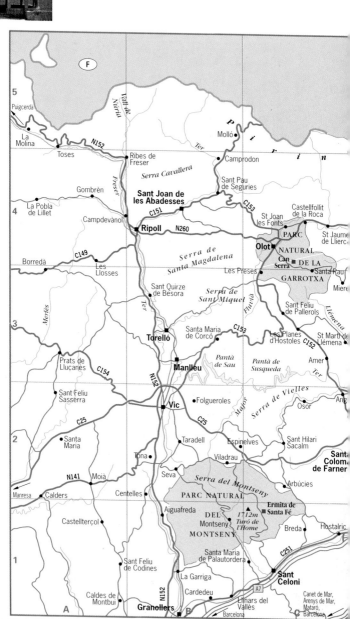

COSTA BRAVA

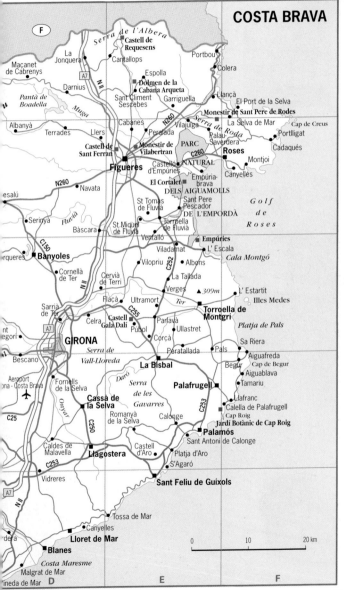

Serra de l'Albera

F

Maçanet de Cabrenys

La Jonquera

Castell de Requesens

Cantallops

Portbou

Colera

Espolla

Dolmen de la Cabana Arqueta

Darnius

Sant Climent Sescebes

Garriguella

Llançà

El Port de la Selva

Pantà de Boadella

Muga

Cabanes

Vilajuïga

Monestir de Sant Pere de Rodes

La Selva de Mar

Cap de Creus

Albanyà

Terrades

Llers

Peralada

Serra de Roda

Palau Saverdera

Portlligat

Cadaqués

Castell de Sant Ferran

Monestir de Vilabertran

PARC

Roses

esalú

Figueres

Castelló d'Empúries

C260

NATURAL

Montjoi

N260

Navata

El Cortalet

DELS AIGUAMOLLS

Empúria-brava

Canyelles

Serinyà

Fluvià

Bàscara

St Miquel de Fluvià

Sant Pere Pescador

DE L'EMPORDÀ

Golf

rqueres

Banyoles

Cornellà de Ter

St Tomàs de Fluvià

Torrpella de Fluvià

Ventalló

Viladamat

de

Roses

Cervià de Terri

Vilopriu

C252

Albons

Empúries

L' Escala

Cala Montgó

Flaçà

Ultramort

La Tallada

Ter

Verges

▲ 309m

L' Estartit

Illes Medes

Sarrià de Te

Celra

Castell Gala Dalí

C255

Parlavà

Torroella de Montgrí

nt egori

A7

GIRONA

Púbol

Corçà

Ullastret

Platja de Pals

Serra de Vall-Lloreda

Peratallada

Pals

Sa Riera

Bescano

La Bisbal

Begur

Aiguafreda

Cap de Begur

Aeroport na - Costa Brava

Fornells de la Selva

Daró

Serra de les Gavarres

Palafrugell

Aiguablava

Tamariu

Onyar

Cassà de la Selva

Llafranc

Calella de Palafrugell

C25

C250

Romanyà de la Selva

Calonge

C253

Cap Roig

Jardí Botànic de Cap Roig

Palamós

Caldes de Malavella

Castell d'Aro

Sant Antoni de Calonge

Llagostera

Platja d'Aro

C253

Vidreres

S'Agaró

A7

Sant Feliu de Guixols

dera

Tossa de Mar

Canyelles

Lloret de Mar

Blanes

Costa Maresme

Malgrat de Mar

ineda de Mar

D

E

F

0   10   20 km

Girona & Central Costa Brava

The craggy coastline of cliffs, coves and cork woods at the heart of the Costa Brava epitomises the nature of the 'Wild Coast'. Tourism has arrived here, but slowly – there are few high-rise hotels, and the villas on the hillsides are mostly second homes for the people of Barcelona. The tranquil resorts around Begur and Palafrugell, with their sandy beaches and shimmering bays, are some of the most relaxing places on the entire Catalan coast. Inland, towns like Besalú and Pals have been restored to their medieval splendour, while the Garrotxa region of sleeping volcanoes around Olot makes for an interesting day out. There are historic castles and monasteries to be explored, and Girona, the provincial capital, is one of the most pleasing cities in Spain.

' The Sardana is the most beautiful of all dances, which join and disjoin; it is a magnificent, moving ring...

JOAN MARAGALL
Catalan poet (1860–1911),
La Sardana

Girona

The capital of the Costa Brava region was founded by the Romans on the site of an Iberian settlement in the 1st century BC. Over the years it has been subject to numerous invasions – Charlemagne liberated it from the Arabs in 785, and Napoleon besieged the city for seven months in 1809. The city you see today consists of a medieval centre built on top of the Roman foundations, and an expanding new town across the Onyar river, whose waterfront houses form the most enduring image of Girona.

You can still make out traces of the old Roman city. Carrer de la Força, the cobbled street at the heart of the Jewish quarter, was once part of the Roman Via Augusta, a continental highway linking Rome to southern Spain. The Sobreportes arch at the foot of the cathedral steps is built over one of the old Roman entrances to the city. The statue of the Virgin of Good Death standing in a niche above the arch is a reminder that in later times prisoners were led through this gate to their execution.

But modern Girona is about more than ancient monuments. It's a thriving university city, with cafés, bookshops and bicycles, and a lively provincial capital, playing its part in the Catalan renaissance. The city has been called Barcelona's little sister. It has all the style of the Catalan capital, but is more intimate and approachable.

The spires of the cathedral and the church of Sant Feliu dominate the skyline

Brightly painted houses are reflected in the river

The domed lantern at the heart of the Arab bath house

What to See in Girona

BANYS ÀRABS (ARAB BATHS)

The so-called Arab Baths are a 13th-century Romanesque creation, based on an earlier Moorish design and influenced by Roman styles. Nevertheless, they are one of the best preserved medieval bath houses in Spain and are definitely worth a visit. The most impressive room is the apodyterium or changing-room, with an octagonal pool at its centre beneath a domed skylight supported by eight columns. From here you can walk through the frigidarium (cold chamber) and tepidarium (warm bath) to reach the caldarium, an early sauna with underground heating.

CALL JUEU (JEWISH GHETTO)

For six centuries until their expulsion in 1492, Girona was home to one of the largest Jewish communities in Spain. At one time up to 1,000 Jews lived in the area around Carrer de la Força, where there was a synagogue, a Jewish school, a ritual bath and a Jewish butcher.

At the centre of the ghetto is the **Centre Bonastruc Ça Porta**. This Jewish museum and cultural centre is named after the founder of the Cabbalist school of Judaism, also known as Rabbi Nahmánides, who was born in Girona in 1194. Cabbalism is a secret system of mysticism, metaphysics and mathematics which claims to read hidden messages into the scriptures. A video, available in several languages, tells the tragic story of Catalonia's Jews, persecuted for 300 years before being finally driven out. Centuries later, this small centre in Girona is providing a focus for the renaissance of Jewish Spain.

- 34B4
- ✉ Carrer del Rei Ferran el Católic
- 🕐 Apr–Sep, Mon–Sat 10–7, Sun 10–2; Oct–Mar, Tue–Sun 10–2. Closed 1 Jan, 6 Jan, Easter Sunday, 25–6 Dec
- 🚫 None
- 💰 Cheap

- 34C3
- 🍴 El Pou del Call, Carrer de la Força 14 (££)

Centre Bonastruc Ça Porta
- ✉ Carrer Sant Llorenç
- ☎ 972 21 67 61
- 🕐 Mon–Sat 10–8, Sun 10–3 in summer; Mon–Sat 10–6, Sun 10–3 in winter
- 🚫 None
- 💰 Cheap

CATEDRAL ✪✪✪

Girona's cathedral is one of the great churches of Spain. Begun in 1312 on the site of an earlier church (and before that a mosque), it has evolved over the succeeding centuries into a triumph of different architectural styles, coming together to create a unifying and satisfying whole.

The best way to approach the cathedral is via the huge rococo staircase leading up to its Renaissance façade, an exquisite piece of stone carving with floral reliefs and sculptures of saints supporting the central rose window. Inside, the cathedral is dominated by its single Gothic nave, at 23m the widest in Europe. Other features to look out for include the 11th-century alabaster altarpiece (a remnant of the earlier church) and the embossed silver canopy above the high altar.

The **Museu Capitular** (cathedral museum) contains an illustrated 10th-century manuscript of the *Beatus*, or Commentary on the Apocalypse and the 11th-century *Tapestry of the Creation*. The ticket to the museum also gives access to the 12th-century Romanesque cloisters, with a view of the original bell tower, Torre de Carlemany, skilfully incorporated into the 14th-century Gothic design.

✚ 34C4
✉ Plaça de la Catedral
🕐 Daily 10–2, 4–7, (10–2, 4–8 in summer)
♿ None
🏷 Free

Museu Capitular
☎ 972 21 44 26
🕐 Jul–Sep, Tue–Sat 10–8, Sun–Mon 10–2; Oct–Jun, Tue–Sat 10–2, 4–6, Sun–Mon 10–2
🏷 Moderate
❓ Good audio commentary on *Tapestry of the Creation*, available in several languages

A tough climb but worth it – the best approach to Girona's cathedral

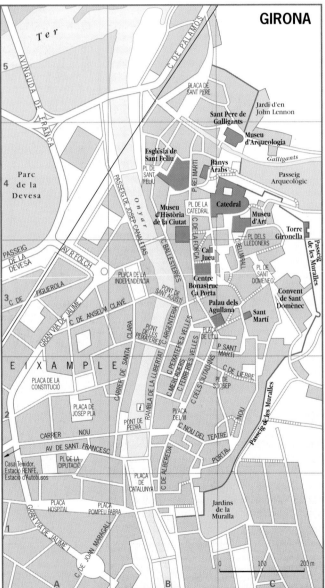

GIRONA

A Walk Around Girona Old Town

This walk is best done during the early evening, when the citizens of Girona take their *passeig* along the Rambla.

Start at the Pont de Pedra, the stone bridge to the north of Plaça de Catalunya. Cross this bridge to reach the old town, continuing into the arcaded Plaça del Vi. Walk across this square and into Carrer dels Ciutadans, once Girona's main thoroughfare.

At this point you could take one of the narrow alleys to your left to explore the medieval streets of the guilds (➤ 20).

Carrer dels Ciutadans leads into Plaça de l'Oli. Turn right to climb the steps to the Jesuit church of Sant Martí.

On the way you pass one of Girona's finest Gothic palaces, Palau dels Agullana.

At the top of the steps, turn left. Cross a small square and climb another set of steps (Carrer de l'Escola Pia) into the heart of the Jewish quarter (➤ 32). A right turn at the top of these steps leads to Carrer Bellmirall.

Cross Plaça dels Lledoners straight ahead to reach the cathedral's southern door on Plaça dels Apòstols. After exploring the cathedral, walk down the flight of steps beneath its main façade into Plaça de la Catedral.

Turn left along Carrer de la Força, the old Roman Via Augusta. Reaching a small square, descend the steps to your right, leading to Carrer de l'Argenteria.

This smart shopping street leads into the Rambla (➤ 38), where you can end your walk with *tapas* and a drink underneath the arches.

Distance
2km

Time
1 hour

Start/end point
Pont de Pedra

✚ 34B2

🚌 1km from bus and railway stations

Tapas
Café l'Arcada (£)

✉ Rambla de la Llibertat 38

☎ 972 20 10 15

Below: *the walk through the old town starts at the Pont de Pedra (bottom)*

34A2

Choice of restaurants and cafés (£–£££)

Girona bus station is in this area

Girona station

EIXAMPLE (NEW TOWN)

Most visitors to Girona spend all their time in the old town to the east of the River Onyar, but the Eixample ('extension'), on the other side of the river, is where most people live and work. This area of town, with its busy ring-roads and modern shops, has little immediate appeal, but an hour or two of exploring can show up some worthwhile sights.

The Plaça de la Independència, where the old town meets the new, is a pleasant 19th-century arcaded square lined with restaurants, cafés and bars. The monument at the centre is to the defenders of Girona, under siege from Napoleon's troops in 1809. A short walk from here leads to the Parc de la Devesa, the city's playground and the largest urban park in Catalonia.

Much of the new town was built in the early years of the 20th century, when the Modernist architectural movement was at its peak. Rafael Masó, born in Girona in 1880, was one of the leading figures in the movement. His Casa Teixidor, with its green ceramic lantern, can be seen on Carrer Santa Eugènia near the station. Designed as a warehouse with flats above, it is now a college of architecture.

Casa Teixidor is Girona's finest example of Modernista (Catalan art nouveau) architecture

Did you know ?

The avenues of plane trees which characterise the Parc de la Devesa have grown to heights of more than 55m. This is because the trees are planted so close together that there is nowhere for them to grow but up. Plane trees from Devesa park were used to line the famous Ramblas in Barcelona.

ESGLÉSIA DE SANT FELIU ✪

Girona's second church is easily recognised by its broken spire, damaged by lightning in 1581 and never repaired. It's an essential feature of the skyline when seen from the Onyar river. Built over the tomb of Feliu of Africa, a 4th-century Bishop of Girona, the church is a mix of architectural styles, from Romanesque to Gothic to baroque. Interesting features include the Roman sarcophagi, both pagan and Christian, built into the sanctuary walls, and the neo-classical chapel of Sant Narcís, with marble walls and painted ceiling.

✚ 34B4
🕐 Variable
🖐 Free

MUSEU ARQUEOLÒGIC ✪✪
(ARCHAEOLOGICAL MUSEUM)

This museum, in the 12th-century Romanesque monastery of Sant Pere de Galligants, contains an interesting collection of artefacts, from prehistoric to medieval times. Among the finds are Roman pottery from Empúries (► 19) and three Roman milestones indicating the distance to Gerunda – the Roman name for the city. The cloister contains a number of headstones from the old Jewish cemetery on Montjuïc hill. The gardens around the back, with their shady fountains and views of the cathedral, would make a lovely spot for a siesta or a picnic.

✚ 34C4
✉ Plaça de Santa Llúcia
☎ 972 20 26 32
🕐 Jun–Sep, Tue–Sat 10:30–1:30, 4–7, Sun 10–2; Oct–May, Tue–Sat 10–2, 4–6, Sun 10–2
♿ None
🖐 Cheap

MUSEU D'ART ✪✪

This museum in the former episcopal palace contains a large collection of Catalan art, from Romanesque to contemporary. Among the exhibits to look for are the 10th-century portable altar from the monastery of Sant Pere de Rodes (► 22), the 14th-century stencils used to design stained-glass windows for the cathedral in Girona, and the scenes of 20th-century Girona by the Catalan artist Santiago Rusinyol and the Polish painter Mela Mutter.

✚ 34C4
✉ Pujada de la Catedral 12
☎ 972 20 38 34
🕐 Mar–Sep, Tue–Sat 10–7, Sun 10–2; Oct–Feb, Tue–Sat 10–6, Sun 10–2. Closed 1 Jan, 6 Jan, Easter Sunday, 25–6 Dec
♿ Very good – wheelchair access and braille panels
🖐 Cheap (free on Sun)

Left: *medieval Romanesque carvings in Girona's art museum*

🔲 34B4
✉ Carrer de la Força 27
☎ 972 22 22 29
🕐 Tue–Sat 10–2, 5–7, Sun 10–2
♿ None
✋ Cheap

MUSEU HISTÒRIA DE LA CIUTAT ⭐

The city museum, in the former Capuchin monastery of Sant Antoni, details the history of Girona from prehistoric times to today. Among the more unusual exhibits, the ground-floor display on industrial history features an old petrol pump, wireless sets and an early computer. Upstairs, there is a room devoted to the development of the *sardana* dance. The cemetery of the original convent is preserved just inside the entrance, with niches on the walls designed for mummified corpses.

🔲 34C2

PASSEIG DE LES MURALLES ⭐⭐

This walkway along the old city ramparts, completed in 1985, offers marvellous views over the city. It begins near the Plaça de Catalunya and continues towards the old convent of Sant Domènec, where another path beside the walls leads to the ruined watch tower, Torre Gironella. You can climb on to this tower for some of the best views, then continue around the ramparts on the Passeig Arqueològic, a series of landscaped gardens between the cathedral and the River Galligants.

Opposite: the monument in Plaça Independència commemorates the defenders of Girona in 1809

🔲 34B2
🍴 Several restaurants and cafés (£–££)
❓ Flower market on Sat; Festa de Sant Jordi; book and flower market, 23 Apr

RAMBLA AND RIU ONYAR ⭐⭐⭐

The Rambla beside the River Onyar is the hub of Girona's social life, and the best place to see it all is from one of the cafés beneath the vaulted arches. The Pont de Pedra, the stone bridge at the top of the Rambla, looks down over the river, with its iron and wooden bridges and brightly painted tenement houses backing on to the water. One of the bridges, the Pont de les Peixateries, cuts directly through the houses and on to the Rambla. It was built for the city by the French firm of Eiffel and Company, creators of the famous tower in Paris.

Below: the bridges across the Onyar connect the old town with the new

What to See in Central Costa Brava

AIGUABLAVA ✪✪✪

It was here, in 1908, that the journalist Ferran Agulló first coined the term *costa brava*, and the rocky coves around Begur retain much of their ruggedness today. Of course they have now been discovered by tourists, and luxury 'urbanisations' are creeping up the hillsides, but out of season you can still have pine-fringed cliffs, golden sand and sparkling turquoise bays (Aiguablava means 'blue water') to yourself. The bay at Aiguablava is dominated, unusually, by an ugly white *parador*, a state-run hotel built on the cliffs to take advantage of the view. Across the bay is the chic resort of Fornells, little more than a marina, a smart hotel and a pair of tiny beaches. North of here are more small coves – Sa Riera, with views over the Medes islands, and Aiguafreda and Sa Tuna, linked by a footpath cut into the rock.

BANYOLES ✪✪

The capital of the Pla de l'Estany county makes a pleasant place to while away a summer afternoon. The main square, Plaça Major, is a perfect example of the genre, with three- and four-storey houses of varying heights and styles climbing above the ground-floor arcades. Just outside Banyoles is a lake, fed by an underground spring, where the 1992 Olympic rowing contests were held. This is where the locals come to have fun in summer – you can swim, fish, rent a rowing boat or walk the 8km around the lake's shore. The jawbone of a pre-Neanderthal man, at least 100,000 years old, was discovered in 1887. A copy is kept in the **Museu Arqueològic**, housed in the 14th-century almshouses in the centre of town.

Sidebar (left column):

✚ 29F2
🍴 Restaurants and bars at Aiguablava, Sa Riera and Sa Tuna (££–£££)
🚌 Buses from Begur to Aiguablava, Aiguafreda and Fornells in summer
↔ Begur (➤ 42), Tamariu (➤ 52)

Below: *the clear blue water at Aiguablava is a magnet for visiting yachts*

✚ 29D3
🍴 Restaurants (£–££)
🚌 Buses from Besalú, Girona and Olot

Museu Arqueològic
✉ Plaça de la Font 11
☎ 972 57 23 61
🕐 Jul–Aug, Tue–Sat 11–1:30, 4–8, Sun 10:30–2; Sep–Jun, Tue–Sat 10:30–1:30, 4–6:30, Sun 10:30–2
♿ None
💰 Moderate

From Banyoles

This drive takes you into the heart of the Garrotxa, the region of dormant volcanoes just inland from Banyoles.

Start by the sports stadium on Carrer Alfonso XII, between central Banyoles and the lake, and take the main road heading north with the lake on your left.

After 4km this road merges with the C150 from Girona. Almost immediately you see the high peaks of the Pyrenees up ahead in the distance. Soon you reach Besalú (► 16): to explore this delightful town, park on the left before the bridge and walk across the medieval Pont Vell.

Leaving Besalú, continue on the main road (now the N260) towards Olot.

After another 13km you see the village of Castellfollit de la Roca (► 44), perched high on a ridge to your left.

Continue through this village. Reaching Olot, take the second exit and skirt the city centre, following signs to Santa Pau.

Shortly after turning on to the Santa Pau road, you see the Can Serra car-park and information centre on your left. If you have time, you could stop here and do the walk described on page 49.

Continue on this winding road to Santa Pau (► 52). After exploring the village, return to the same road as it twists its way down to the plain, with lovely views all the way. Just before entering the hamlet of Porqueres, take the gravel track on your left to reach a 12th-century Romanesque church.

From here you can continue around the shores of the lake to return to Banyoles.

Distance
76km

Time
2 hours plus stops along the way

Start/end point
Banyoles
✚ 29D3

Lunch
Cal Sastre (££)
✉ Placeta dels Balls 6, Santa Pau
☎ 972 68 04 21

Below: *Banyoles – scenes from the lakeside*

41

29F2

Several restaurants and bars (£–££)

Buses from Girona and Palafrugell

Aiguablava (► 40), Palafrugell (► 50), Pals (► 50)

Market on Wed

There are plenty of bargains on the streets of La Bisbal

BEGUR ✪✪

This hilltop town with a ruined 15th-century castle would make a good base for exploring the rocky coves around Aiguablava (► 40). The medieval town centre, with narrow streets fanning out from the church square, is quiet and peaceful by day, but reverberates at night to the sound of funk and salsa music from several lively bars. Many of the houses here were built by wealthy Spanish settlers on their return from the American colonies. From the Mirador Sant Ramon, reached on the climb to the castle, there are views of the coastline stretching north as far as the Bay of Roses.

BESALÚ (► 16, TOP TEN)

29E2

Choice of restaurants and cafés (£–££)

Buses from Girona and Palafrugell

Peratallada (► 50), Ullastret (► 55)

Market on Fri

LA BISBAL ✪✪

La Bisbal is best known as the centre of the Catalan ceramics industry. Its most abiding image – and the only one that many visitors see – is of the dozens of pottery shops lining Carrer de l'Aigüeta on the Girona road. There are good bargains to be had if you shop around, from simple glazed terracotta pots to innovative local designs (► 108). A twin-arched bridge, Pont Vell, leads over the River Daró into the centre of the old town, which comes alive each Friday with one of the region's busiest markets. Wander the narrow lanes and you keep coming across little surprises – a Gothic archway here, a fountain there, a shop selling hand-crafted wooden chairs or a shrine to the Virgin of Montserrat set high into a wall. The Romanesque bishops' palace, on the old town square, is a reminder that this quiet county town was once the seat of the bishops of Girona.

CALELLA DE PALAFRUGELL ✪✪✪

This pleasant resort consists of a series of coarse, sandy beaches strung out beneath an old fishing village. The village now includes a few whitewashed holiday villas, but it has lost none of its original charm. You can still see working fishermen here, and fishing boats on the sand add a splash of colour to the scene. The people of Palafrugell and beyond head to Calella at weekends to eat at the waterfront seafood restaurants, especially during the late winter (Jan to Mar), when sea urchins are on the menu.

Calella de Palafrugell is the setting for one of the Costa Brava's more unusual festivals each July, when popular musicians gather to sing *havaneres* on the beach. These melancholy sea shanties, brought back from Cuba by Spanish sailors and rooted in the Creole music of the Caribbean, have been sung in the fishermen's taverns of Calella for at least 100 years. They are best enjoyed while drinking *cremat*, a local concoction of coffee, rum and cinnamon, which is served flambéed.

A cliff path from Calella leads around to the next bay at Llafranc (► 45). At the other end of the village, high above the bay, is the **Jardí Botànic de Cap Roig**, a beautiful garden laid out in 1927 by a White Russian emigré, Colonel Nicolai Woevodsky, and his English wife, Dorothy Webster. There are cypress, cork oak and mimosa trees and hundreds of Mediterranean plants, tall cedars and pine trees, bent by the wind and leaning towards the sea as if paying homage to the Mediterranean.

🔲 29F2
🍴 Several beachside restaurants (££)
🚌 Buses from Palafrugell
↔ Llafranc (► 45), Palafrugell (► 50)
❓ Festival of *havaneres*, first Sat in Jul

Jardí Botànic
✉ Cap Roig, 4km from village
☎ 972 61 45 82
🕐 Daily 9–8 in summer, 9–6 in winter
💰 Cheap
❓ Costa Brava Jazz Festival held each Jul and Aug

Bottom: *Calella de Palafrugell feels like an old-fashioned resort*
Below: *Jardí Botànic*

Heights don't appear to scare the villagers of Castellfollit de la Roca

CASTELL GALA DALÍ, PÚBOL (➤ 18, TOP TEN)

CASTELLFOLLIT DE LA ROCA ✪✪

Spectacularly perched on a 1km-long basalt promontory, carved out by the River Fluvià, this village looks for all the world as if it is about to fall off the cliff. The best view is from below, as you approach Castellfollit on the road from Besalú. At night, the cliff is floodlit and you can pick out the different geological layers in the rock. The narrow streets of the village, their houses built from volcanic stone, converge by a church, where you can gaze 60m down into the precipice below. Castellfollit is known for its almond biscuits and its pork sausages, and in the **Museu d'Embotits** (Sausage Museum) you can taste the local products after looking at old-fashioned mincing machines and models of the *matança* or annual slaughter of pigs.

L'ESTARTIT ✪

What was once little more than a fishing harbour, serving the nearby town of Torroella de Montgrí (➤ 54), has grown into a bustling, modern holiday resort with a reputation for nightlife and a thriving watersports industry. The main attraction here is the beach, which stretches for 5km and is backed by a seafront promenade. This is a good resort for families with young children – the water is shallow, the sand shelves gently and a miniature train trundles along the seafront. Unlike some of the larger resorts to the south, L'Estartit virtually closes down in winter, when all the locals retreat to Torroella de Montgrí. A popular attraction in summer is a boat trip to the Medes islands (➤ 45), 1km offshore.

 28C4
 Fonda Ca La Paula on main street (£)
🚌 Buses from Besalú, Figueres, Girona and Olot
↔ Besalú (➤ 16), Olot (➤ 46–9)

Museu d'Embotits
✉ Carretera Girona
🕐 Mon–Sat 9:30–1:30, 4–8; Sun 9:30–2, 4:30–8
 Free

➕ 29F3
🍽 Choice of restaurants and cafés (£–£££)
🚌 Buses from Girona and Torroella de Montgrí
↔ Illes Medes (➤ 45), Torroella de Montgrí (➤ 54)

ILLES MEDES (MEDES ISLANDS) ●●●

Seven rocky islets, a continuation of the Montgri massif, harbour a rich diversity of plant and animal life, and in 1985 they were declared Spain's first marine nature reserve. Local fishermen, banned from fishing in the area, feared for their livelihood; but the protection of the marine environment has been such a success that catches are up everywhere else as a result. Scuba divers come from all over Spain to swim among coral reefs and caves teeming with grouper, scorpion fish and spiny lobsters. Glass-bottomed boats leave regularly in summer from the harbour at L'Estartit (► 44); some trips include the opportunity to go snorkelling. There are strict regulations about fishing, boating and night diving in the protected area, and it is essential to check with the authorities at the harbour in L'Estartit. In the past the islands have been used as a pirate hideout and a French military prison, but nowadays they are uninhabited – apart from the sea birds, especially the thousands of yellow-legged gulls, who breed here between March and May each year.

☩ 29F3
🚢 Boat trips from L'Estartit in summer and occasionally on winter weekends
↔ L'Estartit (► 44)

Above: *the view of Llafranc and Calella de Palafrugell from Cap de Sant Sebastià*

LLAFRANC ●●

Pine trees shade a beachfront promenade and yachts flutter in the small marina beside a perfect bay, where tamarisks grow out of the rocks around an arc of fine sand. Although this resort has grown more popular in recent years, the development is restrained and few of the buildings are more than two or three storeys high. A coastal path leads to Calella de Palafrugell (► 43), or you can walk or drive up to the lighthouse at Cap de Sant Sebastià for views back down over Llafranc.

☩ 29F2
🍴 Several good restaurants (££)
🚌 Buses from Palafrugell
↔ Calella de Palafrugell (► 43), Palafrugell (► 50), Tamariu (► 52)
❓ Festival of *havaneres* on the beach, first Sat in Aug; annual festival, 29–31 Aug

45

Olot

The capital of the Garrotxa region is a truly Catalan town which manages to be both industrious and stylish, conservative at heart with a radical edge. The people of Olot have a strong sense of Catalan identity: you are unlikely to hear anyone speaking Spanish. This Catalan spirit is openly displayed at the town's two biggest festivals – the *Aplec de la Sardana*, on the second Sunday in July, when visitors come from all over Catalonia to perform the *sardana* dance; and the *Festa de la Tura*, on 8 September, when figures of giants and hobby-horses parade through the streets.

Olot was a centre of textile production, and an art school was opened here in the 18th century. A century later, one of its pupils, Joaquim Vayreda, helped to found the Olot School of painters. The romantic scenes of rural life produced by these early Catalan impressionists were influenced by the European trends of the time, yet rooted in the Garrotxa landscape of volcanic hills. Artists are still coming to Olot today, and a descendant of Joaquim Vayreda has a gallery in the old quarter.

The smart shopping streets of the old town around the Plaça Major lead to the neo-classical parish church of Sant Esteve. Near here is the start of the Rambla, also named Passeig Miquel Blay, after a well-known Olot sculptor. This delightful promenade, with coffee tables beneath the trees, contains some unusual Modernist architecture, as well as the 19th-century Teatre Principal.

There are good views over Olot's rooftops from the surrounding volcanic hills

Left: *Garrotxa stone church*
Below: *the path to Montsacopa*

What to See in Olot

CASAL DELS VOLCANS (HOUSE OF VOLCANOES)

The Garrotxa region around Olot has been at the centre of volcanic activity for hundreds of thousands of years. Although the most recent eruption was more than 11,000 years ago, the volcanoes are still officially considered dormant, rather than extinct. Nor are volcanoes the only threat. A major earthquake struck the city in 1427, and there were tremors at nearby Besalú as recently as 1988. This museum, housed in a Palladian villa inside the botanic gardens at Parc Nou, explores the history and geology of the volcanic region, as well as its fauna and flora. The information centre for the Garrotxa natural park, in an office above the museum, is a good place to pick up leaflets about the area and walking maps and guides.

A waymarked walk (No 17) from the museum leads to the Volcà de Montsacopa, a typical volcano just north of the town centre. You can get there just as easily by following the signs from the Museu Comarcal, from where it will take around 20 minutes to reach the crater. Pass market gardens on the lower slopes, then walk uphill through an avenue of plane trees lined with Stations of the Cross. From the chapel of Sant Francesc, on the summit, there are marvellous views back down over Olot's rooftops and over the surrounding landscape, carved out by volcanic activity. You can walk right around the rim of the crater, or follow the path down to its floor. Another path leads to the crater of Volcà de la Garrinada, 500m away.

+ 28C4

✉ Avinguda de Santa Coloma (1km from town)

☎ 972 26 62 02

ℹ (in museum): Jul–Sep, Mon, Wed–Sat 9–2, 5–7, Sun 9–2; Oct–Jun, Mon, Wed–Sat 9–2, 4–6, Sun 9–2

🍽 None   ♿ Good

Did you know ?

At one stage there were 15 factories in Olot producing religious sculpture for markets in Europe and the USA. The largest factory, El Arte Cristiano, was founded by Joaquim Vayreda in 1880. The factory is still in business, on the street that bears his name. A bust of Vayreda stands near by, facing his old family home.

✚ 28C4
✉ Carrer Hospici 8
☎ 972 27 91 30
⏱ Mon, Wed–Sat 11–2, 4–7, Sun 11–2
🍴 Near by (£–££)
♿ Good
🎫 Cheap

Below: *Modernist architecture on La Rambla*

✚ 28C4
✉ Carrer Dr Zamenhoff
☎ 972 26 91 84
⏱ Daily 9–9
🎫 Moderate

MUSEU COMARCAL DE LA GARROTXA
(GARROTXA COUNTY MUSEUM)

An 18th-century hospice houses this museum, which contains the most important collection of work from the Olot School of painters. Key figures in the movement were Josep Berga i Boix (1837–1914) and Joaquim Vayreda (1843–94). Many of Vayreda's paintings of rural life are on display, together with others by his brother Marià, better known as a writer. The Modernist sculptor Miquel Blay was also influenced by the Olot School; among his works is a portrait of Berga i Boix. More modern work includes a selection of nudes by the sculptor Josep Clarà, a pupil of Berga i Boix. The museum also includes displays on Olot's traditional industries – bell-making, clog-making, textiles and religious statuary.

MUSEU INTERACTIU ✪

Olot's newest tourist attraction is this 'interactive museum' above a petrol station on the edge of town, where more than 10,000 species of Pyrenean bird and animal, together with sound and light effects, can be summoned to your computer screen at the touch of a button. A good place to take the children on a rainy day.

Volcanic Walk near Olot

This easy-to-follow walk provides an excellent introduction to the volcanic landscape around Olot and takes in three of its best-known features. There are no regular buses to the start of the walk, so it is best to arrive by car or bike, or on a tourist carriage from Santa Pau.

Start at the Can Serra car park, 5km out of Olot on the Santa Pau road. There is an information centre here where you can pick up a map of the walk in summer. Cross the road and descend the steps into the Fageda d'en Jordà beech wood.

The entire walk is waymarked with the symbol of two walkers on a red background and the number 1. It continues through this shady wood, situated on a lava flow, before emerging beside a yoghurt factory and climbing to the 11th-century church of Sant Miquel de Sacot.

Follow the waymarks. A steep climb leads to the summit of the Santa Margarida volcano, from where an optional circular path heads down into the crater, with a small hermitage at its centre.

The Santa Margarida volcanic crater

The path now descends to the main road, passing a farm where you can buy drinks and snacks.

Cross the road and take the lane which leads past the Santa Margarida restaurant, skirting the Volcà del Croscat. Until recently this volcano was quarried for its stone, and another optional path (No 15) leads to the scarred cliff-face to see the dramatic effects of the quarrying.

Continue around this volcano, passing a piggery, and return through more beech woods to Can Serra.

Distance
10km plus optional extras

Time
3–4 hours

Start/end point
Can Serra
✚ 28C4

Lunch
Restaurant Santa Margarida (£)
✉ Opposite Lava campsite on the GI524
☎ 972 68 02 70

Right: *medieval Pals*
Below: *detail carved in Palafrugell cork*

🔢 29E2

🍴 Choice of restaurants (£–££)

🚌 Buses from Girona and nearby beaches

↔ Begur (➤ 42), Calella de Palafrugell (➤ 43), Llafranc (➤ 45)

❓ Market on Sun; Spring Festival, Whit Sunday; annual festival, 19–21 Jul

🔢 29E3

🍴 Choice of restaurants and cafés (££)

🚌 Buses from Palafrugell

↔ Begur (➤ 42), Peratallada (➤ below)

PALAFRUGELL ⭐⭐

A growing community of British expatriates has been attracted to this busy market town on the edge of the Lower Empordà plain. They are drawn to its down-to-earth Catalan atmosphere and to the excellent nearby beaches. It was once an important centre of cork production, and the Museu del Suro (cork museum) has some interesting displays on the history of the cork industry, as well as a selection of artefacts made from cork. The best time to visit Palafrugell is on Sunday, when the streets fill with stalls for one of the region's liveliest markets.

PALS ⭐⭐

This walled village of Gothic stone houses around a 15th-century castle was abandoned in 1939 after the Spanish Civil War, but it was slowly and lovingly restored after 1948. Many of the houses are now second homes for people from Barcelona. At times the village is too pretty for its own good – numerous galleries and pottery shops testify to its popularity with tourists – and to appreciate it at its best you should come in the early morning or the evening, when the sunlight is at its most subtle and you can enjoy the alleys and archways without the crowds. The long, sandy beach of Platja de Pals, with modern holiday facilities, is 5km away on the coast.

🔢 29E3

🍴 Choice of restaurants and cafés (£–£££)

↔ La Bisbal (➤ 42), Pals (➤ above), Ullastret (➤ 55)

PERATALLADA ⭐

A bridge leads across the original moat to this medieval village, whose name means 'hewn stone', and the cobbled alleyways are full of stone houses bearing ancient coats of arms. People travel for miles at weekends to eat in Peratallada's restaurants, the most famous of which is inside the 11th-century castle at the centre.

RIPOLL ✪✪✪

Wilfred the Hairy, the first Count of Barcelona, used Ripoll as a base from which to unite the rival factions of the southern Pyrenees, following the reconquest of Catalonia from the Moors. He founded the Monestir de Santa Maria in 879 on the site of an earlier Visigothic church. During its golden age in the 11th and 12th centuries, the monastery ruled over an area stretching from Barcelona into modern France and became a great centre of European learning. Most of the church was destroyed by fire during the dissolution of the monasteries in 1835, but the great west portal survived. This is one of the jewels of Catalan Romanesque architecture, its pillars and arches covered in vivid reliefs of Biblical stories, zodiac signs and scenes from agricultural life. The 12th-century cloisters of the monastery church have also survived, with expressive faces on the sculpted capitals. The nearby **Museu Etnogràfic** has everything from matchboxes and cowbells to Civil War posters gathered together by a local historian.

✚ 28B4
🍽 (£–££)
🚌 Buses from Girona and Olot
↔ Sant Joan de les Abadesses (► below)
❓ Market on Sat; wool festival, first fortnight in May

Museu Etnogràfic

✉ Plaça Abat Oliba
☎ 972 70 31 44
🕐 Tue–Sun 9:30–1, 3:30–7:30 in summer; Tue–Sun 9:30–1, 3:30–6 in winter
♿ None
🎟 Cheap

SANT JOAN DE LES ABADESSES ✪✪

The convent was established by Wilfred the Hairy as a gift for his daughter Emma, whom he appointed the first abbess. The 9th-century original has been replaced with a 12th-century Romanesque church, whose greatest treasure is its carved wooden Calvary. Other sights in this attractive town, a good place to break a journey between Ripoll and Olot, include a strangely pointed bridge over the River Ter and the church of Sant Pol, with a tile sculpture of *sardana* dancers among the ruins.

✚ 28B4
🍽 Cafés and bars (£)
🚌 Buses from Ripoll
↔ Ripoll (► above)
❓ Market on Sun

The old bridge over the River Ter leads into Sant Joan de les Abadesses

🗓 28C3

🍴 Cal Sastre, Placeta dels
Balls (££)

🚌 Occasional buses from
Banyoles and Olot

↔ Olot (➤ 46–9)

*Above: Tamariu, where
the trees reach down to
the beach*

🗓 29F2

🍴 Seafood restaurants
(££–£££)

🚌 Buses from Palafrugell in
summer

↔ Aiguablava (➤ 40),
Llafranc (➤ 45)

❓ Festival of *havaneres* on
the beach, first Sat in Sep

SANTA PAU ⭐⭐

The tourist capital of the Garrotxa region has at its heart a
fortified medieval enclave with a well-restored baronial
castle. The centre of the village is closed to traffic, so it is
best to park outside and walk in through the original
gateway, Portal Nou. Plaça Major, the main square, is as
attractive as any in Catalonia, with wooden balconies,
stone arcades and the Romanesque church of Santa
Maria. The castle, first built in the 14th century, is in the
neighbouring square, Placeta dels Balls. A short walk from
here is the Portal del Mar i Mirador, giving panoramic
views over the Garrotxa valleys and a distant glimpse of
the sea. Santa Pau is an excellent base for exploring this
volcanic region – you can follow numerous well-marked
footpaths, hire a mountain-bike or a horse, take a ride in a
horse-drawn carriage or fly over the volcanoes in a
helicopter or a balloon.

TAMARIU ⭐⭐

Named after the tamarisk trees that once surrounded its
bay, Tamariu is the smallest and prettiest of the three
resorts on this stretch of coastline near Palafrugell. In
recent years it has become decidedly chic, and many of
the old fishermen's cottages have been turned into holiday
homes for Catalan families from Girona and Barcelona.

The main beach, a crescent of golden sand, is backed
by a wide pedestrian promenade lined with seafood
restaurants. A short walk around the headland to the
north leads to the rocky cove of Aigua-xellida, with its own
small beach.

A Circular Walk from Tamariu

This walk begins with a short stretch of rocky coastline, before heading inland for the gentle climb to the summit of Puig Gruí (154m).

Start on the beach at Tamariu. From the southern end of the beach, near the car-parking area, cross to the smaller beach of Platja dels Liris and climb the steps, marked with red and white stripes, to join the GR92 coastal path.

You have to scramble across one rocky cove and climb around the next before levelling out on to a path running behind a stone wall.

At the next cove, climb for a few metres, then turn left through a wood of tamarisk trees. Continue to follow the red and white waymarks.

Eventually the path curves to the right, following the bend in the sea, then zigzags down to the beach at the tiny cove of Cala Pedrosa.

Take the path directly behind the beach, climbing through the valley; at the top of this path turn right (leaving the GR92) to reach a road. Turn left along this road. After 50m, take the track on your right, just after a crossroads sign. The path is now marked with yellow and white stripes.

Passing an old well, you climb through a tamarisk wood, with occasional glimpses of the sea to your right, until you reach the summit of Puig Gruí.

Keep to the waymarks. The path drops steeply through the forest until it reaches a road with a wide circle. Turn right and continue on this road to return to Tamariu.

Distance
8km

Time
2½ hours

Start/end point
Tamariu
✚ 29F2
🚌 Buses from Palafrugell in summer

Lunch
Es Dofí (££)
✉ Passeig del Mar 22, Tamariu
☎ 972 62 00 43

On the coast path near Tamariu

29E3

Cafés and bars in the town centre (£)

Buses from L'Estartit, Figueres, Girona and Palafrugell

L'Estartit (➤ 44)

Market on Mon; international music festival, Jun–Aug; Festa de Santa Caterina, Sun before 25 Nov

Museu del Montgri i del Baix Ter

Carrer Major 31

972 75 73 01

Apr–Sep, Mon, Wed–Sat 10–2, 6–9, Tue and Sun 10–2; Oct–May, Mon, Wed–Sat 10–2, 5–7, Tue 10–2

None

Free

TORROELLA DE MONTGRÍ

This delightful town of Gothic palaces, courtyards and narrow streets comes alive each Monday as the weekly market spills out in all directions from the porticoed main square, Plaça de la Vila. Stalls are piled high with local cheeses and sausages in this spot, where the *sardana*, the modern Catalan folk dance, was danced for the first time. The nearby **Museu del Montgrí i del Baix Ter** has interesting displays on local history, geology and wildlife. Recent archaeological excavations have revealed the presence of elephants, bears and rhinoceroses here in palaeolithic times. A steep climb from the town centre leads to the Castell del Montgri, built in 1294 and recently restored, standing guard over the town on the limestone Montgrí massif. Just below the castle, in a pretty valley, is the hermitage of Santa Caterina, scene of a pilgrimage and *sardana* festival each November.

Above: *gothic Torroella, in the shadow of the Montgrí castle, has a lively Monday morning market (right)*

ULLASTRET ★★

Archaeological excavations at Ullastret have revealed most of what we know about the ancient Iberian culture, which thrived here between the 6th and 2nd centuries BC. It developed in the late Bronze Age as a result of contact between early Greek settlers and native populations, and is considered to be the first indigenous culture of modern Spain. The Iberians were the first Spanish people to develop a written language; they learnt pottery and metallurgy, and established towns and trading centres.

The Iberian settlement at Ullastret is the largest yet discovered in Catalonia. This fortified village was built on what was, at that time, an island on a marshy lake, but is now at the centre of a fertile plain of olive and almond groves. Parts of the walls and the defensive towers remain, together with public buildings including cisterns, grain stores and a pair of temples to an unknown god. Most of the remains date from around the 3rd century BC; they were probably built over the foundations of earlier houses. The village was abandoned in the 2nd century BC, following the Roman occupation of Empúries (➤ 19), and was deserted until excavations began in 1947.

A museum in the former chapel of Sant Andreu interprets the remains and contains finds from the excavations. There is a model of the site, and the displays describe the Iberian lifestyle (hunting, fishing, quarrying, metalwork), the development of money and of trading with the Greeks, the mysterious language which has still not been deciphered, and the rituals of cremation and child burial, which hint at the possibility of child sacrifice.

✚ 29E3
✉ Site: Puig de Sant Andreu
☎ 972 17 90 58
🕐 Site: Jun–Sep, Tue–Sun 10–8; Oct–May, Tue–Sun 10–6; museum: Jun–Sep, Tue–Sun 10–8; Oct–May, Tue–Sun 10–2, 4–6
🍴 None
♿ Access to museum, but the site is uneven
💵 Cheap
↔ La Bisbal (➤ 42), Peratallada (➤ 50)

Ullastret, an early centre of Iberian civilisation

In the Know

If you only have a short time to visit Costa Brava, or would like to get a real flavour of the region, here are some ideas:

10

Ways to Be a Local

Try to learn a few words of Catalan – people really appreciate it, and it can make a big difference.

Relax, take your time and settle into the Mediterranean pace of life. The Catalans may be more industrious than other Spaniards but they still know how to take it easy.

Take a siesta to avoid the afternoon sun – have a long lunch instead, or fall asleep in the shade.

Put on your best casual clothes and join in the evening *passeig*, strolling along a seafront promenade or the Ramblas in Figueres and Girona.

Do everything late – a late lunch, a late supper, a very late night.

Find out when Barcelona are playing football on television and head for the local bar – you won't be alone.

Join in the *sardana* dance, often performed in village squares after church on Sundays – the dancers hold hands in a circle, and anyone can join in.

Go topless on the beach if you like but don't wander around town in your swimwear.

Respect the local environment – don't pick wild flowers or leave litter on the beaches.

The signs here are in Catalan, not Spanish

The sardana is the symbol of Catalan unity

Remember that you are in Catalonia as well as Spain. Many locals do not consider themselves Spanish, and the Spanish language is referred to as *castellano* (Castilian).

10

Good Places to Have Lunch

Bahía (££), Passeig del Mar 19, Tossa de Mar ☎ 972 34 03 22. Great seafood overlooking the beach.

Boira (£–££), Plaça Independència 17, Girona ☎ 972 20 30 96. *Tapas* downstairs and a restaurant upstairs with romantic views over the river.

El Bulli (£££), Cala Montjoi, Roses ☎ 972 15 04 57. Simply the best restaurant on the Costa

Brava, and a fabulous setting too. Booking essential.

Can Manel (££), Passeig Marítim, Llançà ☎ 972 38 01 12. Catalan home cooking with an emphasis on local seafood.

Can Salvi (££–£££), Passeig del Mar 23, Sant Feliu de Guíxols ☎ 972 32 10 13. Fishy specialities on the seafront promenade.

Curia Reial (££), Plaça Llibertat, Besalú ☎ 972 59 02 63. Hearty meat dishes served along with a violin accompaniment on a terrace overlooking the medieval bridge.

Durán (££), Carrer Lasauca 5, Figueres ☎ 972 50 12 50. Top-notch Catalan cooking in Salvador Dalí's old haunt.

Mas Oliver (££), Avinguda d'Espanya 68, Palafrugell ☎ 972 30 10 41. Country cooking in a large house on the edge of town, with a children's play area in the garden.

Mesón del Conde (£–££), Plaça Major, Sant Martí d'Empúries ☎ 972 77 03 06. The best of the restaurants in this pretty village square near the ruins at Empúries.

El Port (£–£££), Esplanada del Port, Blanes ☎ 972 33 48 19. Fresh fish from the neighbouring market beneath the harbour walls.

10
Activities

Diving and snorkelling: especially around the Medes islands (➤ 45).

Fishing: licences for sea-fishing are issued by local tourist offices.

Golf: there are seven courses in the Costa Brava (➤ 114).

Horse-riding: there are centres in most of the main resorts, with tuition for beginners and more advanced riders.

Sailing: there are 17 marinas between Blanes and Portbou, ranging from Aiguablava (62 moorings) to Empúria-brava (4,000).

Skiing: La Molina and Vall de Núria are popular winter sports centres in the Pyrenees, near Ripoll.

Swimming: the Costa Brava's beaches are perfect for safe swimming.

Walking: on the GR92 coastal path, or inland in the volcanic Garrotxa region or the Albera mountain range.

Waterskiing: available at all of the main resorts.

Windsurfing: all along the coast, and especially around the Gulf of Roses.

10
Top Family Beaches

- Blanes
- Empúria-brava
- L'Estartit
- Lloret de Mar
- Palamós
- Platja d'Aro
- Platja de Pals
- Roses
- Sant Feliu de Guíxols
- Tossa de Mar

5
Great Coastal Views

- Cap de Creus
- Cap de Sant Sebastià, Llafranc
- Castell de Sant Joan, Blanes
- Castell de Sant Salvador, above Monestir de Sant Pere de Rodes
- Ermita de Sant Elm, Sant Feliu de Guíxols

Above: *cool off in summer with a spot of waterskiing*
Left: *ancient dignity blends with modern style in Tossa de Mar*

The North Coast & Beyond

This region stretches from the wide Gulf of Roses, with its marshes, estuaries and endless beach, to the wild northern coastline, where the Pyrenees drop into the sea. Foreigners have long been drawn to these shores – it was here that the Greeks and Romans established their first ports – and the area around trendy Cadaqués has become the most fashionable stretch of the Costa Brava.

The north coast is inextricably linked with Salvador Dalí, whose surreal landscapes owe much to the scenery around Cap de Creus. Take the twisting coast road from Portbou to El Port de la Selva, with the mountains on one side and the sea on the other, then drive across the headland, with its wind-sculpted rocks, and you soon see how the artist and the landscape were made for each other.

'Catalans! September 11, 1714–1938'

ANON
Poster celebrating Catalan
autonomy, Spanish Civil War (1938)

───────●───────

Looking down over El Port de la Selva

Figueres

The capital of the Alt Empordà region would be just another county town, were it not for the influence of its most famous son, Salvador Dalí. Tourists pour in by the busload to see his surreal theatre-museum (▶ 25) and Figueres is enjoying a new-found prosperity as a result. For centuries it was an unassuming market town, created by royal charter in 1267; now it is firmly established on the Spanish tourist circuit.

Long before Dalí's birth in 1904, Figueres had a reputation for creativity and new ideas – federalism, Republicanism, Modernist art. The Utopian socialist Narcís Monturiol, claimed as the inventor of the submarine, was born in the same street as Dalí; it was another local resident, Pep Ventura, who created the modern form of the *sardana* in the mid-19th century.

What to See in Figueres

➕ 29E4
🍴 Restaurants and bars (£–££)

Below: *Dalí's surreal monuments draw many visitors to Figueres*

BARRI ANTIC (OLD TOWN)　　　　　　　😊😊

Between the Rambla and the Dalí museum lies the centre of old Figueres, now a network of pedestrian shopping streets. Several of these streets converge on Plaça Ajuntament, a peaceful, arcaded square that was once the gateway to the city. The street names leading away from the square show Figueres' historical importance as the

crossroads of northern Catalonia – Carrer Girona to the south, Carrer Besalú to the west, Carrer La Jonquera to the north and Carrer Peralada to the east.

CASTELL DE SANT FERRAN ✪✪

This star-shaped citadel, begun in 1753 as a defence against the French, was once claimed to be the second-largest fortress in Europe. During the Napoleonic Wars it was captured by French forces, who imprisoned and later executed the hero of the Girona resistance, Alvarez de Castro. From 1904 to 1933 it was a high-security prison, holding some of Spain's most dangerous criminals.

The castle is still in military use, but parts of it, including the vaulted stables, have recently been opened to the public. Even when it is closed you can get a feel for its vast size by walking around the 3km path that encircles the castle walls.

29E4

✉ 1km out of the city on Carrer de Sant Ferran

☎ 972 50 26 53

🕐 Daily 10:30–8 in summer; Tue–Fri 10:30–1, Sat and Sun 10:30–1, 4–6 in winter

♿ None

✋ Cheap

🚌 Shuttle 'train' service from Teatre-Museu Dalí in summer

MONESTIR DE VILABERTRAN ✪

In the village of Vilabertran, 2km from Figueres, is an Augustinian abbey which is considered to be one of the finest examples of Catalan Romanesque architecture. The 11th-century basilica, with three aisles, three apses and a tall, square belltower, still stands, together with a 12th-century cloister with plant motifs carved on its capitals. In summer the abbey is the setting for a delightful series of classical music concerts. Among the other buildings are the original chapter house and wine cellar, and a 15th-century Gothic abbots' palace.

29E4

✉ On the road from Figueres to Peralada

🔄 Peralada (► 67)

❓ Summer music festival, Jun–Jul

Below: the castle walls
Below left: Modernista art

Right: *the monument at the top of La Rambla to Narcís Monturiol, inventor of a submarine*

➕ 29E4
✉ Rambla 2
☎ 972 50 23 05
🕐 Tue–Sat 11–7, Sun 10–2
♿ Few
 Cheap

➕ 29E4
✉ Carrer Sant Pere 1
☎ 972 50 45 85
 Moderate

➕ 29E4

MUSEU DE L'EMPORDÀ ✪

The museum of local art and history was established in 1876 and moved to its present site on the Rambla in 1971. It contains archaeological discoveries from the Iberian, Greek and Roman periods, and a collection of 19th- and 20th-century Catalan art. There are several paintings by Antoni Tàpies, a Dalí and a lithograph donated by Joan Miró. Artists from Figueres are well represented in the section on Empordan realism. On the ground floor, a room is devoted to Narcís Monturiol, inventor of a submarine.

MUSEU DE JOGUETS (TOY MUSEUM) ✪✪

In the old Hotel Paris, this museum started from one man's collection. Over 3,000 traditional toys are displayed, from cardboard horses to nativity scenes (➤ 111).

RAMBLA ✪✪

The heart of Figueres is its Rambla, a tree-lined boulevard built over an old stream with small squares at either end. Whenever he was far from home, Dalí used to reminisce about Figueres' Thursday market, and the pavement cafés on the Rambla on market day are still the best place to take the pulse of the town. There are two good museums here, and several Modernist houses, designed by local artist, Josep Azemar. Near by, in Plaça Josep Pla, is the Cine-Teatre Jardí, a spectacular *Modernista* theatre, built in 1914.

Did you know ?

Figueres was the last bastion of Republicanism in Spain after Barcelona fell to the Nationalists in January 1939. The Republican parliament held its last meeting in the Castell de Sant Ferran (➤ 61) on 1 February that year.

Around Figueres

Start at the station. Cross the small park of Plaça Estació and fork right along Carrer Pompeu Fabra.

Turn right at the end of this street to reach the old grain market, Plaça del Gra, where a market is still held on Thursdays. Cross this square and take Carrer Concepció to reach Plaça de la Palmera. Turn left and continue towards the Rambla.

A statue of Narcís Monturiol dominates the Rambla's eastern end. Walk down the central avenue, then take Carrer Lasauca, ahead on the left, passing the Hotel Durán, an old Dalí haunt. Cross the ring road at the end of this street to reach the tourist office in Plaça del Sol.

Continue along Carrer Mestre Falla. Take the first right to reach Parc Bosc, a shady and peaceful retreat from the crowds flocking to the Dalí museum. After exploring the park, return to Passeig Nou, where you entered, and turn left. Cross the main road again and take Carrer Pep Ventura straight ahead.

Emerging on Pujada del Castell, look left for your first glimpse of the Dalí museum. Cross this street into Carrer Besalú. To visit the museum, turn left along Carrer Sant Pere; otherwise, continue straight ahead into the town hall square, Plaça Ajuntament.

Cross this square and take Carrer Peralada to reach the large, ochre-coloured Modernist building, Casino Menestral, with a restaurant on the ground floor. Turn right on to Carrer Ample, then left at the end of this street to return to Plaça de la Palmera and retrace your steps to the station.

Distance
2km

Time
1 hour

Start/end point
Figueres station
✚ 29E4
🚌 Buses to Figueres bus station on Plaça Estació
🚉 Trains from Girona and Portbou

Lunch
Durán (££)
✉ Carrer Lasauca 5
☎ 972 50 12 50

The evening passeig (stroll) is a Catalan ritual

Cap de Creus is one of Spain's wild places

 29F4

Restaurant Cap de Creus (££)

Cadaqués, 8km away

Cadaqués (► 17), Portlligat (► 68)

 Sardana dancing at sunrise on 1 Jan

What to See on the North Coast & Beyond

CADAQUÉS (► 17, TOP TEN)

CAP DE CREUS ✪✪✪

This jagged peninsula, where the Pyrenees jut into the sea, is a place of savage beauty and vicious winds. Salvador Dalí lived just down the road at Portlligat (► 68), and as you stand on the headland gazing down into secluded creeks it is impossible not to see Daliesque images in the rocks, carved by nature into ever more surreal shapes. This is where the *tramuntana*, the legendary north wind that strikes fear into sailors and fishermen, is at its most violent. If you come when the wind is blowing you will struggle to stay on your feet.

The easiest way to reach the cape is from Cadaqués (► 17), on a narrow road which snakes across the headland. There is also a coastal footpath from Portlligat, difficult to follow but with the reward of seeing this craggy landscape at its isolated best and dipping into hidden coves along the way. The road ends at a lighthouse, where you can walk on to the slate cliffs and look down over the seascape of deep turquoise water, small islands and rocky coves. This is the easternmost point in mainland Spain and if you come here at dawn you can watch the sun rise over the Iberian peninsula. Sea birds migrate here in winter and wheatears and rock thrushes build their nests in spring, when the cliffs are carpeted with wild flowers and the headland is scented with rosemary and lavender. Swifts and pipits arrive in summer. In 1998 the entire headland was designated a protected nature reserve.

CASTELLÓ D'EMPÚRIES ✪✪

So often when travelling in the Costa Brava you come across an attractive town of cobbled lanes, Gothic mansions and back-street cafés set back just a few kilometres from the sea. Castelló d'Empúries was the seat of the Counts of Empúries during the Middle Ages and many of its buildings date from that time. Its greatest glory is the basilica of Santa Maria, an early Gothic church built on the site of a Romanesque cathedral and considered the second church of Girona province, after Girona Cathedral itself. It is worth visiting just to see the magnificently sculpted portal; inside there is a Romanesque double font and a fine alabaster altarpiece by Vicenç Borràs. Other buildings of note are a 14th-century prison and the El Rentador wash-house, with a porticoed atrium, a fountain and a view of the basilica through its arches.

The nearby resort of Empúria-brava was built in 1967 on the Muga river delta. It consists of a large marina and an extensive network (30km) of canals, plus hundreds of near-identical whitewashed holiday villas, each with their own private mooring. There is a long beach and facilities for every kind of watersport, as well as boat trips on the canals and around the coast. There is even a small aerodrome offering parachuting and pleasure flights. The resort is well laid-out and undeniably attractive, but lacks any authentic Catalan feel.

The decision to build Empúria-brava on former marshland led indirectly to the creation of the Aiguamolls de l'Empordà nature reserve (► 23).

🚏 29E4

🍴 A few restaurants and bars in the town (£–££); many more in Empúria-brava (£–£££)

🚌 Buses from Cadaqués, Figueres and Girona

🔵 Parc Natural de l'Aiguamolls de l'Empordà (► 23), Roses (► 24), Figueres (► 60–3), Peralada (► 67), Sant Pere Pescador (► 70)

❓ Market on Tue; La Verge de Candelera, 2 Feb; Diada del Carme festival at Empúria-brava, 16 Jul; Festa de Sant Llorenç, 10 Aug; Terra dels Trobadors (minstrel festival), 11 Sep

The basilica at Castelló d'Empúries stands out among the sunflowers

COLERA

This small resort close to the French border has two large pebble beaches set into a horseshoe bay, with a fishing harbour at one end. A flight of steps from the northern beach leads to the Art Parc, where you can clamber over a collection of brightly coloured tile sculptures. Near here is the tiny train station. A road from the station leads to the next bay at Cala Rovellada, with its own small beach.

EMPÚRIES (► 19, TOP TEN)

L'ESCALA

What was once just a fishing port has grown into a major holiday resort. There are several good beaches to either side of the town, especially at Cala Montgó to the south. Anchovies have been salted here ever since the Greeks landed at nearby Empúries (► 19); local sardines are another good buy at the fish auctions which still take place by the harbour each weekday afternoon.

LLANÇÀ

Llançà was built 2km back from its harbour in an effort to deter pirates, with the result that it is neatly split into two parts. The old town is largely unaffected by tourism; life centres around the Plaça Major, with its outdoor cafés, Romanesque belltower and Baroque parish church. The busy harbour, with beaches to either side, has a pleasant promenade lined with fish restaurants. Climb the rocky outcrop on the edge of the marina for great views of Cap de Creus (► 64) poking out to sea.

MONESTIR DE SANT PERE DE RODES (► 22, TOP TEN)

PARC NATURAL DE L'AIGUAMOLLS DE L'EMPORDÀ (► 23, TOP TEN)

PERALADA   ✪✪

The moated Renaissance castle that dominates this village is better known these days as Catalonia's most stylish casino (► 113). Entrance to the castle museum, with its collections of glass and ceramics and the largest private library in Spain, also gives access to the 14th-century Carmelite convent within the castle walls. Also of interest is the Romanesque cloister of Sant Domènec and the arcaded main square, Plaça Major. Peralada lies at the centre of the Empordà–Costa Brava wine demarcation and the current owners of the castle, the Mateu family, produce some excellent wines.

EL PORT DE LA SELVA   ✪✪

With its whitewashed houses facing an attractive harbour, this small resort on the edge of the Cap de Creus peninsula looks every bit the timeless Mediterranean fishing village that it almost is. Fishing boats still set out each day to gather the anchovies for which El Port de la Selva is known, but fishing is slowly giving way to tourism. The water is shallow, the beach is long and sandy, and there is good windsurfing in the sheltered bay. The Serra de Roda mountains, with the monastery of Sant Pere de Rodes (► 22) looking down, provide the perfect backdrop.

From Llançà (opposite) the views stretch as far as El Port de la Selva (above)

🕂 29E4
🍴 Several good restaurants (££)
🔁 Figueres (► 60–3), Castelló d'Empúries (► 65), Serra de l'Albera (► 71)
❓ International music festival in the castle grounds, Jul–Aug

🕂 29F5
🍴 Restaurants and bars on the waterfront (£–££)
🚌 Buses from Cadaqués, Figueres and Llançà
🚢 Boat excursions to Cap de Creus
🔁 Monestir de Sant Pere de Rodes (► 22), Llança (► 66)
❓ Market on Fri

Glimpses of a tortured genius – Dalí's house at Portlligat

29F4

🍴 Restaurants at Hotel Portlligat and Aparthotel Calina (££)

📷 Cadaqués

↔ Cadaqués (➤ 17), Cap de Creus (➤ 64)

Casa-Museu Dalí

☎ 972 67 75 00

🕐 15 Jul–15 Sep, daily 10:30–9; 15 Mar–14 Jun and 16 Sep–6 Jan, Tue–Sun 10:3–6

✋ Expensive

❓ Advance booking is essential

29E5

🍴 Restaurants on waterfront (££)

🚆 Trains from Figueres and Girona

↔ Colera (➤ 66)

PORTLLIGAT ⭐⭐

This small fishing village on the outskirts of Cadaqués (➤ 17), with boats moored on the beach and the gentle waters of the bay enclosed by an offshore island, is where the painter Salvador Dalí made his home. He first moved here with his future wife Gala in 1930 and stayed permanently from 1948 until her death in 1982. His house, **Casa-Museu Dalí**, built over the ruins of a pair of fishermen's cottages, contains typical Dalíesque touches – eggs on the roof, camels in the garden and a swimming pool modelled on the Alhambra in Granada. It is now open to the public, largely as Dalí left it, and a visit here provides a fascinating insight into the artist's troubled mind. Dalí campaigned successfully for Portlligat and neighbouring Cadaqués to be spared the excesses of mass tourism. If only he could see Portlligat in summer, when visitors have to queue to get into his house.

PORTBOU ⭐

'Benvinguts' ('Welcome'), says a sign in Catalan at the entrance to this town, leaving day-trippers from France in no doubt that they have arrived in Catalonia, as well as Spain. The opening of the international railway station in 1878 transformed this fishing village into a busy transport hub and there is now a road across the border as well, to the French port of Cerbère. High-speed trains from Paris to Barcelona will eventually pass through Portbou. At the centre of town, the Rambla de Catalunya is an attractive tree-lined boulevard and there is another pretty promenade in front of the pebble beach.

A Dalí Drive from Portlligat

This drive takes in all the major sights associated with the life of Salvador Dalí, beginning at his home in Portlligat and ending at his final resting-place in Figueres. It also re-creates the macabre journey made by Dalí's chauffeur, Artur Caminada, on 10 June, 1982, with the body of Dali's wife, Gala, in the back seat. She had stipulated that she wanted to die in her castle at Púbol and when she died at Portlligat instead it was Caminada's job to carry her 'home'.

Begin by the beach in Portlligat (➤ 68) and follow signs to Cadaqués (➤ 17). Just before reaching Cadaqués, turn right towards Roses.

Continue on this road as it winds across the cape, bypassing Roses to head towards Figueres.

Shortly after passing Castelló d'Empúries on your right, take the left turn for Sant Pere Pescador (➤ 70).

You now cross the Empordan plain, passing through a succession of small towns and villages. The road, signposted to La Bisbal, goes through Torroella de Fluvià, Viladamat, Verges and Ultramort before reaching Parlavà.

Turn right at the traffic lights in Parlavà. Reaching the Girona road, turn right again and take the next left to visit the Castell Gal Dalí, Púbol (➤ 18). After visiting the castle, return to the Girona road. Before reaching Girona, turn right on to the N11 towards Figueres.

This road runs parallel to the motorway towards France with occasional glimpses of the Pyrenees to your left. After 30 minutes, take the exit for Figueres. The Dalí museum (➤ 25) is in the centre of town.

Dalí drew inspiration from the fishing boats on the beach outside his house

Distance
115km

Time
2½ hours plus lunch and visit to Castell Gala Dalí, Púbol

Start point
Portlligat
✚ 29F4

End point
Figueres
✚ 29E2

Lunch
Can Bosch (£)
✉ Púbol
☎ 972 48 83 57

✚ 29E4

🍴 Restaurants and bars
(£–££)

🚌 Buses from L'Escala,
Figueres and Palafrugell

↔ Parc Natural de
l'Aiguamolls de
l'Empordà (➤ 23),
Castelló d'Empúries
(➤ 65)

ROSES (➤ 24, TOP TEN)

SANT PERE PESCADOR ✪✪

The village of 'St Peter the Fisherman' was built 3km back from the sea to provide a safe haven from pirates, with the unforeseen result that it has largely escaped the Costa Brava's tourist boom. While other fishing ports have been transformed into mass-market, modern resorts, Sant Pere Pescador remains a peaceful, workaday place, where farmers and fruit-growers mingle with occasional foreign tourists on the banks of the River Fluvià.

There is a 17th-century baroque church and the remains of an old castle, but the real attraction of Sant Pere Pescador is its beach, a long and lonely stretch of sand on the shores of the Gulf of Roses. There are no high-rise hotels here, just campsites among the dunes; come out of season when the campsites are closed and you can have sweeping views of the bay all to yourself.

The coastline is protected from development by being part of the Aiguamolls de l'Empordà natural park (➤ 23). The protected area also includes the banks of the Fluvià, on both sides of the village. You can walk along well-marked paths to reach the Illa de Caramany, a wooded island and bird reserve created when the course of the river was diverted in 1979.

Close to Sant Pere Pescador are a number of interesting medieval villages, rising above the flat Empordan plain. Sant Miquel de Fluvià is best known for its 11th-century Romanesque abbey, while Sant Tomàs de Fluvià also has an 11th-century priory church, with recently discovered murals.

Windsurfers at Sant Pere Pescador

The Albera mountains are dotted with megalithic monuments and tombs

SERRA DE L'ALBERA ✪✪

The Albera mountain range, on the French border, is where the Pyrenees begin their long descent into the sea. It is a place of frontier villages and mountain passes, of vineyards, olive groves and cork forests and, in the north, a natural park which offers excellent walking along tracks once used by smugglers and refugees.

The park's information centre is at Espolla, a village of narrow streets huddled around a church. Espolla is at the heart of the Costa Brava's wine industry, and at co-operatives outside the village you can taste and buy the local *Vi de l'Empordà*. The area around Espolla is also known to archaeologists as the place with the greatest concentration of megalithic monuments in Catalonia, with tombs, rock carvings and standing stones dating back to 3500 BC. One of the easiest to reach is the Dolmen de la Cabana Arqueta, a burial chamber between Espolla and the next village of Sant Climent de Sescebes. Other paths from Espolla lead to the Dolmen del Barranc, with human and animal figures carved into the roof, and to the standing stones at Rabós d'Empordà, from where a mountain track leads to the 11th-century monastery of Sant Quirze de Colera.

A hair-raising drive from Sant Climent, best attempted in an off-road vehicle, snakes across the mountains to the Castell de Requesens, a restored medieval castle on the site of an earlier fortress. A good road from here, through the village of Cantallops, leads to the border crossing at La Jonquera, where lorries thunder past on the motorway from Paris to Barcelona.

🚩 29E5
🍴 Restaurants in Espolla and Sant Climent (£–££)
🚌 Bus from Figueres to Espolla
🔁 Peralada (➤ 67)

Food & Drink

Catalan cooking is one of the great cuisines of Europe, with the produce of the sea and the mountains enhanced by many foreign influences. The Romans introduced olives and planted vines; the Arabs brought saffron, almonds and dried fruit. The essential flavours are Mediterranean – olive oil, garlic, onions, tomatoes, peppers – and the latest trend towards 'modern Catalan' cuisine combines traditional ingredients with French and Italian styles.

Main Meals

The most characteristic style of cooking is known as *mar i muntanya* (mountain and sea). This produces unusual combinations, like chicken with lobster, rabbit with snails and pigs' trotters stuffed with prawns. Paella comes into this category too – a mound of steaming saffron rice which might be topped with just about any combination of meat, seafood and snails.

Meat is always excellent, especially veal from Girona and lamb from Ripoll. Duck might be accompanied by either turnips or pears. One famous meat dish is *escudella i carn d'olla*, a hearty boiled meat casserole which is traditionally served at Christmas; the broth is eaten with pasta shells as a starter, with the meat to follow. The Catalans are particularly proud of their many pork sausages: popular varieties include *botifarra, bisbe, llonganissa* and *fuet*. Some are eaten raw, like a salami, but *botifarra* is usually grilled and served with white beans.

The seafood along the Costa Brava is always mouth-wateringly fresh

Fish and seafood are served all along the coast, often simply grilled with a *romesco* (tomato, almond and pepper) sauce. Hake, monkfish and sole are widely available; seabass and mullet are more expensive. *Suquet de peix* is a delicious casserole of white fish and potatoes, poached in white wine.

Snacks, Salads and Starters

Tapas bars (▶ 95) serve a bewildering range of snacks, from meatballs to octopus, in saucer-size portions. The classic bar snack is a plate of *pa amb tomàquet* – bread rubbed with tomato, drizzled with olive oil and topped with thin slices of cheese or cured mountain ham. Most bars keep a selection of *truitas* – cold potato omelettes, sometimes flavoured with spinach, artichoke or courgette. A Catalan salad *(amanida)* makes a meal in itself – piles of lettuce, tomato, olives and onions with a selection of cold meats, cheeses, tuna and egg. Other popular starters include *escalivada* (grilled pepper and aubergine salad) and *esqueixada*, a salad topped with shredded salt cod.

Desserts

Spain is not known for its desserts but Catalonia produces two of the best – *crema catalana*, an egg custard with a caramelised sugar crust, and *mel i mató*, curd cheese with honey. In most eating places you are likely to be offered a choice between fresh fruit, ice-cream and *flan* (caramel custard).

Tapas bars are the best places to snack out

Catalan Wine

The red and white wines from the Penedès region south of Barcelona are some of the best in Spain and usually offer excellent value. Torres' *Etiqueta Negra* (Black Label), from this region, is one of the great red wines of the world. Most Catalans drink red wine *(vi negre)* or rosé *(vi rosat)* rather than white *(vi blanc)* – unless they are drinking *cava*, Spain's answer to champagne, which also comes from this region. The Costa Brava produces its own wine, known as *Vi de l'Empordà*, in the Alt Empordà region around Peralada. *Vi Novell* is a young, fruity red, bottled immediately after the harvest, and *Garnatxa* is the local dessert wine.

The South Coast & Beyond

Anyone who visited the Costa Brava in 1950 would not recognise this region today. Huge concrete resorts have been created out of little more than fishing harbours, and in summer the coastline reverberates to the sound of the disco beat. Resorts like Lloret de Mar and Platja d'Aro led the way into mass tourism and they are still among the busiest in Spain.

Not everywhere on the south coast is like this. Sant Feliu de Guíxols and Tossa de Mar are also popular resorts, but their old towns retain a lot of charm. Towns like Blanes and Palamós are still fishing ports as well as tourist centres. And even on the most crowded stretches of coastline it is still possible to find a hidden cove, a reminder of what the Costa Brava used to be before the tourists took over.

'The Catalans are neither French nor Spaniards, but distinct people, both in language, costume and habits...'

RICHARD FORD
A Handbook for Travellers in Spain
(1855)

———————●———————

Platja d'Aro

BLANES ✪✪✪

Blanes is where it all begins. The Costa Brava starts at Sa Palomera, a rocky promontory halfway along the beach, and continues north all the way to France. Once used for shelter by the town's fishing fleet, the promontory has the remains of an old fire-tower – a primitive lighthouse – at its summit and it is still lit up by fire each year during the Costa Brava's international fireworks contest in July.

Climb on to Sa Palomera, passing the fishing boats which are washed up on the shingle beach, for some of the best views of Blanes. South of here, the beach stretches on, as far as the eye can see, passing hotels, campsites and the mouth of the River Tordera at the start of the Costa Maresme (➤ 79). To the north, a wide promenade with gardens, play areas and restaurant tables on the street leads around to the town's attractive, and still busy, fishing harbour.

Blanes is still a working fishing port, where the arrival of the fleet each evening is followed by an animated auction in the fish market – you can watch it all happening from the upstairs bar. Fishermen mend their nets, old men sit on the sea walls and the sailors' chapel of Nostra Senyora de l'Esperança is adorned with nautical themes. Blanes may be one of the Costa Brava's largest resorts, but with a

A daily auction still takes place each afternoon beside the fishing harbour at Blanes

population of more than 20,000 it has managed to absorb the tourists without losing its soul.

The old town, just behind the seafront, has survived almost unscathed, with Gothic churches, medieval houses, fountains, shrines and a lively daily produce market. Out of season this is a real Catalan town, best experienced during the sunset promenade when everyone from grandmothers to tiny children put on their best clothes and stroll beside the sea.

Just above the town is the **Mar i Murtra** botanic garden, dramatically situated on a clifftop. There is a splendid collection of South American cactus plants, plus Californian and Chilean palms, spiny aloe from South Africa and a charming Mediterranean garden with olive, pine and tamarisk trees dropping down towards the sea. From the Linnaeus rotunda you can look down over a small cove of sparkling turquoise water and cliffs where the bushes grow wild out of the rocks. This is a very special and peaceful place, even for those who have little interest in plants. You can walk around the guided trail in less than an hour, but you could easily spend a day here, with a good book and a picnic, enjoying the sun and the shade and the sound of the sea.

The road beyond the gardens continues to the small beach and former tuna-fishing port at Cala Sant Francesc, where there is a beach bar in summer. You can also walk or drive from the gardens to the Castell de Sant Joan, an 11th-century castle and 15th-century hermitage with sweeping views of the town's beach.

Opposite: *The 11th-century castle of Sant Joan perches on a hill, looking down over Blanes*

+ 29D2

🍴 Restaurants and bars (£–££)

🚌 Buses from Girona and Palafrugell

🚂 Trains from Figueres and Girona

❓ Market on Tue

Below: one of the spa hotels in Caldes de Malavella

CALDES DE MALAVELLA ⭐⭐

This market town, 15km south of Girona, has been famous for its hot springs since Roman times: recent excavations uncovered the remains of two Roman spas. The town enjoyed a revival during the mid-19th century, when it took advantage of the European fashion for 'taking the waters'. Dr Modest Furest marketed its bottled water under the name Vichy Catalán – a name seen on mineral water bottles throughout Spain to this day. People still come to Caldes to take the waters at the two spa hotels, built around the turn of the 20th century in neo-classical and Modernist style. They offer a range of health and beauty treatments and are particularly recommended for those with digestive and respiratory disorders. Caldes is a the centre of the wooded Selva landscape and would make a good base for a healthy walking, cycling or riding holiday.

+ 29E2

🍴 Restaurants and bars in Sant Antoni de Calonge (£–££)

🚌 Buses from Girona, Palafrugell and Palamós

↔ Palamós (➤ 82), Platja d'Aro (➤ 82)

❓ Markets: Calonge, Thu; Sant Antoni de Calonge, Wed

CALONGE ⭐

The old village of Calonge is split into two parts: the medieval centre, 2km from the sea, dominated by its Gothic castle; and the modern tourist resort of Sant Antoni de Calonge, with hotels, villas and campsites strung out along the coast road between Palamós and Platja d'Aro. From the village there are some pleasant drives through forests of cork and holm oak – north to La Bisbal (➤ 42), or west to Romanyà de la Selva, where a 4,000-year-old burial chamber stands in a lonely spot in the woods, surrounded by a stone circle.

COSTA MARESME ✪✪

The 'marshy coast', which runs south from Blanes, is very different in character from the Costa Brava. Nobody would call this rugged – this is a narrow, flat coastal strip, where the beaches are mostly artificial and the villages are cut off from the sea by a busy highway and railway line. The resorts here are mainly used by weekend visitors from Barcelona, though the area's popularity with German tourists has also earned it the nickname *Costa dels Alemanys*. Behind the coast the countryside is known as Catalonia's market garden, where fruit and vegetables and the region's famous carnations are grown.

The coastal highway begins just south of Blanes, near the town of Malgrat de Mar. Next comes Pineda de Mar, where the remains of a Roman aqueduct can be seen. The road continues through a succession of old fishing villages,

- ✚ 29D1
- ▣ Trains from Blanes to most of the resorts
- ▤ Boats from Blanes to Calella de la Costa in summer
- ↔ Blanes (► 76–7)
- ❓ Markets: Arenys de Mar, Sat; Caldes de l'Estrac, Fri; Calella de la Costa, Sat; Canet de Mar, Wed; Malgrat de Mar, Thu; Pineda de Mar, Fri; flower market at Vilassar de Mar, Mon–Wed 3–6

now almost completely given over to tourism. Sant Pol de Mar is an attractive village with a marina, sandy beaches and a 12th-century hilltop monastery, while Canet de Mar is known for its Modernist architecture. Arenys de Mar is still a working fishing port, with a daily fish market by the harbour and a shady Rambla leading up to the town. Near here is Caldes d'Estrac, a spa town since Roman times. Finally you reach Mataró, the capital of the region; beyond here are the suburbs of Barcelona. South of Mataró, at Vilassar de Mar, is the flower market where the florists along Barcelona's Ramblas come to buy their wares.

Sant Pol de Mar, 10km south of Blanes on the 'marshy coast'

LLORET DE MAR ✪✪✪

Fifty years ago Lloret de Mar was still a fishing village; now it has been transformed into a pulsating resort whose population rises to 200,000 in summer and where it is easier to get a hamburger than a Spanish meal. The main thoroughfare, Carrer la Riera, is a non-stop strip of discos, bars and amusement arcades, busy day and night. During the 1990s there have been attempts to change Lloret's image, but that seems to be missing the point. If you want fun in the sun, there's no better place.

The main attraction is the beach. The best sheltered swimming is at the north end, beneath the mock castle on the smaller beach of Sa Caleta. Several more beaches are within easy reach – Cala Gran and Cala Canyelles to the north, Platja de Fenals and Santa Cristina to the south. This last is the setting for a traditional festival each July, when the people of Lloret make a pilgrimage by boat, carrying a statue of their patron saint to the hermitage bearing her name. The old town lies just behind the promenade. Look for the 16th-century parish church, with its unusual *Modernista* tiled roof.

🔹 29D1
🍴 Wide choice of restaurants and bars (£–£££)
🚌 Buses from Blanes, Girona and Tossa de Mar
⛴ Boats to other south coast resorts in summer
↔ Tossa de Mar (► 26), Blanes (► 76)
❓ Market on Tue; Festa de Santa Cristina, 24–6 Jul

Below: *Lloret de Mar's Modernist church and mock castle (bottom)*

A Coastal Drive from Lloret de Mar

This drive takes in the most dramatic stretch of coast road in the Costa Brava.

Start at the car park at the north end of the beach, beside the sardana statue. Take the road that leads uphill, away from the sea, and turn right at the traffic lights towards Tossa de Mar.

Once you leave Lloret the road begins to climb, and there are various *miradors* where you can pull over and admire the sea views. After passing through Tossa de Mar (➤ 26) the road twists and turns through a dizzying series of bends, with cork woods to your left and cliffs dropping into the sea on your right.

Follow this coast road for 20km from Tossa de Mar, then turn right into Sant Feliu de Guíxols (➤ 84). Turn left along the seafront and left again, following signs to Platja d'Aro. Pass through the centre of this resort (➤ 82) and continue for another 5km to Sant Antoni de Calonge, where you turn left towards Calonge (➤ 78).

From Calonge a minor road winds its way through the forest to the pottery town of La Bisbal (➤ 42).

Reaching La Bisbal, turn right towards Palafrugell. Keep on this road as it bypasses Palafrugell and continues south towards Palamós (➤ 82).

Keep going south on the coast road from Palamós, retracing your route from Sant Antoni de Calonge. The views along the corniche from Sant Feliu to Tossa are completely different when seen from the other direction.

Distance
130km

Time
3–4 hours

Start/end point
Lloret de Mar
✚ 29D1

Lunch
Bahia (££)
✉ Passeig del Mar 17, Sant Feliu de Guíxols
☎ 972 32 02 19

The cliffs plunge sheer into the sea along the coast road from Tossa to Sant Feliu

PALAMÓS ✪✪

This fishing port at the eastern end of Palamós bay was founded in 1277 and soon became an important naval base: when the Aragonese fleet conquered Sicily in 1299, it sailed from Palamós. In the 19th century Palamós was the chief export harbour for Catalonia's cork industry, and despite the growth of tourism the town retains a significant commercial base today. The fishing fleet still sails each day from Palamós and its arrival each afternoon is followed by a lively fish auction by the harbour.

The old quarter, dominated by the Gothic church of Santa Maria, stands on a headland overlooking the harbour. Several shops here specialise in cork artefacts from the continuing small-scale cork industry. The modern town has gradually extended along the waterfront, with hotels and apartment blocks to the south and a tree-lined promenade. To the north of Palamós are a pair of good sandy beaches, Platja de la Fosca and Platja de Castell.

⊞ 29E2

🍴 Restaurants (£–£££)

🚌 Buses from Girona, Palafrugell and Platja d'Aro

📷 Boats to other south coast resorts in summer

↔ Calonge (► 78), Platja d'Aro (► below)

❓ Market on Tue; carnival, week before Lent; Mare de Déu del Carme, procession of fishing boats on 16 Jul

The resort of Palamós is still a working fishing port

PLATJA D'ARO ✪✪

The small fishing harbour of the village of Castell d'Aro has grown over the last 50 years into the Costa Brava's second largest resort, with a population that rises from 3,000 in winter to more than 100,000 in summer. The beach is 3km of golden sand; the nightlife is legendary and there are numerous activities for children. From discos to watersports, whatever you want in Platja d'Aro is probably there – except peace and quiet.

The original village survives 3km inland, with a medieval castle where art exhibitions are sometimes held, and a Museu de la Nina (Doll Museum, ► 111). For those who want to escape from the beach, there are free guided walking tours of the old village throughout the year.

⊞ 29E2

🍴 Wide choice of restaurants (£–£££)

🚌 Buses from Girona, Palamós and Palafrugell

📷 Boats to other south coast resorts in summer

↔ Calonge (► 78), Palamós (► above), S'Agaró (► 83)

❓ Market on Fri; carnival, week before Lent

S'AGARÓ ✪✪

This exclusive villa development, on a headland between the beaches of Sant Pol and Sa Conca, was begun around 1924, when industrialist Josep Ensesa commissioned Girona architect Rafael Masó to design the first houses. Built in his classical *noucentista* style, the resort is an

29E2
🍴 Beachside restaurants at Platja Sant Pol (££); Hostal de la Gavina (£££)
↔ Platja d'Aro (► 82), Sant Feliu de Guíxols (► 84)

attractive mix of Italianate villas, landscaped gardens and delightful coastal promenade around a succession of rocky coves. Masó's work was completed in the 1940s by Francesc Folguera, who designed the neo-baroque church at the centre of the resort. Film stars and politicians have long flocked to S'Agaró's famous hotel, Hostal de la Gavina, designed by Masó as a Gothic villa and given a more austere classical style by Folguera. Like the rest of the resort, the hotel is elegant and attractive, but has an air of exclusivity which can be off-putting.

Above: *Cala Sa Conca, at the northern end of S'Agaró*
Inset: *Platja d'Aro, nightlife capital of the Costa Brava*

➕ 29E1
🍴 Restaurants (£–£££)
🚌 Buses from Girona,
Palafrugell and Palamós
🚢 Boats to other south
coast resorts in summer
↔️ Platja d'Aro (➤ 82),
S'Agaró (➤ 83)
❓ Market on Sun; carnival
procession, Sun before
Lent; Mare de Déu del
Carme, procession of
fishing boats on 16 Jul

Museu Municipal
✉️ Carrer Abadia
☎️ 972 82 15 75
🕐 Jun–Sep, Tue–Sat 11–2,
6–9, Sun 11–2; Oct–May,
Tue–Sat 11–2, 5–8, Sun
11–2
✋ Cheap

*The horseshoe arches of
the Porta Ferrada*

SANT FELIU DE GUÍXOLS ⬤⬤⬤

This used to be the Costa Brava's busiest resort. It's an unexpectedly handsome and dignified town, where most of the building took place before the 1960s high-rise boom. Fishing and boat-building are important industries, and during the 19th century the town grew rich on the export trade in cork. The elegant Modernist buildings on the seafront are a reminder of this wealth: look out for Casino la Constancia, a Moorish-style edifice with arches, mosaics and turrets and an old-style café on the ground floor.

Sant Feliu grew up around its Benedictine monastery, of which all that remains is the Porta Ferrada, a pre-Romanesque atrium with horseshoe arches. The same complex of buildings includes the parish church, built over the monastery ruins, and a small museum (**Museu Municipal**) of local artefacts and archaeological finds.

The main beach is a wide arc of sand with a fishing harbour at its north end. From the beachfront promenade, Rambla Vidal leads into the old town of narrow streets and squares. The market square contains an unusual 1929 market hall, with art deco touches and bright stained glass. From the southern end of the beach, a road climbs 2km to the chapel of Sant Elm. A tourist 'train' runs up here regularly in summer.

SERRA DE MONTSENY ⭐⭐

The Montseny mountain range is an attractive region of cork, pine and beech forests, villages and mountain streams, straddling the border between Girona and Barcelona provinces, just inland from the southern Costa Brava. It's known throughout Spain for its springs: much of the country's mineral water is bottled here, especially in the spa town of Sant Hilari Sacalm.

There are two routes into the Serra de Montseny from the coast. Both involve heading for the A7 motorway, which you can leave at the junctions for either Hostalric or Sant Celoni. A circuit of the region, beginning at Hostalric and returning via Sant Celoni, would make a good full-day excursion from one of the south coast resorts.

Hostalric is a medieval walled village, perched on a basalt rock and surrounded by cork forests; a short drive west leads to Breda, known for its pottery shops. The road continues north to Arbúcies, where there is a museum of local crafts in the porticoed town square, before snaking through the mountains to the charming village of Viladrau. From here there is a choice of routes south to Sant Celoni – one via Seva, through the village of Montseny itself, the other passing the region's highest peak, Turó de l'Home (1,712m). At the hermitage of Santa Fé, beneath Turó de l'Home, there is an information centre and a choice of several waymarked walks. Here you are at the heart of the Serra de Montseny nature reserve, and you may see peregrines, eagle owls and red squirrels.

TOSSA DE MAR (► 26, TOP TEN)

🕇🍴 28B2
Restaurants in all the towns and villages (£–£££)

🚌 Buses from Girona to Sant Hilari Sacalm

🔁 Vic (► 86–90)

❓ Markets in Arbúcies, Breda and Sant Hilari Sacalm, Sun; Living Via Crucis, re-enactment of Christ's crucifixion on Good Friday, Sant Hilari Sacalm; Enramades, ancient festival of floral art on the Sun after Corpus Christi, Arbúcies; Festa del Flabiol, flute festival in Arbúcies, late Oct

Above: *Hostalric is one of several attractive Catalan towns and villages in the Serra del Montseny*

Vic

The opening of the C25 highway, tunnelling through the north of the Montseny mountain range from Girona, has brought the ancient market town of Vic within easy reach of the coast. This is a town known even among Catalans as the essence of Catalonia, with an attractive medieval centre containing architecture from Roman to Modernist, enclosed by a ring road on the site of the old city walls.

Market day in Vic is a great time to meet the locals

The best time to visit Vic is on a market day (Tuesday or Saturday), when the main square, Plaça Major, is buzzing with life. Fruit and vegetables are sold at one end, flowers at the other, while the arcades around the edges shelter everything from baby chicks to second-hand books. Stalls at the centre of the square sell bric-à-brac, pottery, household utensils and cheap clothes, and a New Age craft market is set up in the neighbouring square, Plaça del Pes. The fishmongers and sausage-makers on Carrer dels Argenters do a brisk business (Vic has long been renowned for its *fuet* and *botifarra* sausages) and the streets of the old town echo with gossip. By 1:30PM the bars are full and the market has been cleared away; by 4PM the cleaners have done their job, the cafés have put out their chairs and you can sit in the sun and appreciate Plaça Major as it is the rest of the week, with pigeons in the square, children playing in the sand and no sign that a market has taken place at all.

What to See in Vic

CATEDRAL ⊘⊘

Vic's cathedral was begun in the 11th century, but the present building dates from 1803, when the Romanesque belltower was incorporated into a new neo-classical design. Parts of the original cloister survive, with a 14th-century Gothic cloister on top. The most unusual feature is the set of wall paintings by the Catalan mural artist Josep Maria Sert. His first paintings were damaged by fire during the Spanish Civil War and the replacements were inaugurated only days before his death in 1945. The striking red and gold colours and apocalyptic Biblical scenes form a powerful link between the persecution suffered by Christ and that felt by Catalonia at the hands of Spain. Sert is buried in the cloisters. A few of the remaining pieces from his first decoration of the cathedral are displayed in the Capella Fonda, a baroque chapel on Carrer Cardona.

✠ 28B2
✉ Plaça de la Catedral
🕐 Daily 10–1, 4–7
♿ None
🎫 Free

Below: *Josep Maria Sert's striking paintings adorn the walls of Vic's cathedral*

MUSEU DE L'ART DE LA PELL (LEATHER MUSEUM) ⊘

Tanning is one of Vic's traditional industries, and this museum, housed in a bright, modern building, contains an unusual collection of leather artefacts from around the world. There are chopstick holders from China, funerary face masks from Cameroon, embossed armchairs from Portugal and a riding saddle from Mexico all collected by Andreu Colomer i Munmany. For some reason a pianist plays as you walk around. A real treat.

✠ 28B2
✉ Carrer Arquebisbe Alemany 5
☎ 938 83 32 79
🕐 Tue–Sat 11–2, 5–8, Sun 11–2. Open till midnight on Wed in Jul–Aug
♿ Good
🎫 Free

> ### Did you know ?
> *Markets have been held twice a week in Plaça Major ever since the 10th century. The biggest market, Mercat del Ram, takes place on the Saturday before Palm Sunday, when elaborately decorated palm fronds are on sale, accompanied by sardana dancing and the selection of a palm queen.*

MUSEU EPISCOPAL ✪✪

The diocesan museum contains more than 17,000 exhibits, including the most complete collection of Catalan Romanesque art outside Barcelona. The collection is currently awaiting rehousing in a new purpose-built museum and for the next few years only a small selection of works will be on display, in the Gothic hall of the Holy Cross Hospital. The emphasis is on religious art, with Romanesque and Gothic altarpieces and wooden statuary from local churches.

➕ 28B2
✉ Rambla de l'Hospital 52
☎ 938 85 64 52
🕐 15 May–14 Oct, Mon–Sat 10–1, 4–6, Sun 10–1; 15 Oct–14 May, daily 10–1
♿ Separate access and parking
✋ Cheap

PLAÇA MAJOR ✪✪

Vic's main square is one of the most perfect in Catalonia, where buildings of different styles and ages come together, linked by the uneven arches around their base, to create a satisfying whole. This has always been, above all else, a market place; but to experience the symmetry and beauty of the square you need to come back when it is empty. To one side stands the Gothic town hall, begun in 1388; around the square are buildings from the Renaissance, baroque and Modernist periods.

➕ 28B2
🍴 Cafés and bars around the edge (£)

Opposite and below: *Vic's Plaça Major is like a history of Catalan architecture*

A Walk around Vic

Distance
3km

Time
1½ hours

Start/end point
Vic station
✚ 28B2
🚌 From Girona to nearby
bus station

Lunch
La Taula (££)
✉ Plaça Don Miquel de
Clariana 4
☎ 938 86 32 29

The city authorities have created a *ruta turística* around the old town of Vic. By following this simple walk you get to see all the city's main monuments in a short space of time.

Start at the railway station (the bus station is 100m from here). Walk down Carrer de Jacint Verdaguer, directly opposite the station entrance, leading to Plaça Major.

The tourist office is close to the town hall, directly ahead of you on the far side of the square. If it is open, pick up the leaflet about the town trail, with descriptions of the various buildings along the way. If not, simply follow the signs marked *Ruta Turística*.

Follow the route by heading down Carrer de la Ciutat behind the town hall, then turning right on to Carrer Miquel de Sants.

Continue on this route as it passes historic houses and baroque churches, as well as a Romanesque bridge, a section of the old city walls and a 2nd-century Roman temple. Eventually you return to Plaça Major, where you can stop for a coffee before returning to the station by a different route.

Carrer dels Argenters, the lane at the corner of the square, is home to bakers, butchers and delicatessens

Go down Carrer dels Argenters, the narrow lane in one corner of the square with Forn Sant Miquel on the corner. Reaching a small square, turn left into Carrer de les Escales and go down the steps to reach Rambla del Passeig. Turn left and follow the Ramblas along the course of the old city walls. Turn right when you reach Carrer de Jacint Verdaguer to return to the station.

Where To...

Above: *Bisbal pottery
is world famous*
Right: *fresh
seafood is always
on the menu*

Girona

Prices

Prices are approximate, based on a three-course meal for one without drinks and service:

£ = under 2,000 ptas
££ = 2,000–4,000 ptas
£££ = over 4,000 ptas

Most restaurants serve a *menú del día* at lunchtime, which will usually work out a lot cheaper. It is normal practice to add about 10 per cent to the bill as a tip.

Albereda (£££)

Formal restaurant serving inventive, modern Catalan cuisine, with traditional ingredients prepared in low-fat, healthy sauces. Probably the best restaurant in the old town.

✉ **Carrer Albereda 7** ☎ **972 22 60 02** 🕐 **Lunch Mon–Sat and dinner Tue–Sat**

L'Arcada (£)

Tapas bar snacks downstairs, a restaurant upstairs and tables outside on the Rambla. This is a popular meeting-place, with live salsa late on Thursdays and jazz on Fridays.

✉ **Rambla de la Llibertat 38** ☎ **972 20 10 15** 🕐 **7AM–1AM daily**

L'Argado (££)

The speciality at this bustling restaurant, close to Devesa Park, is barbecued meat, such as chicken, veal and sausages cooked on a charcoal grill.

✉ **Avinguda Ramon Folch 7** ☎ **972 22 13 03** 🕐 **Lunch and dinner daily**

El Balcó (££)

This Argentinian restaurant is a paradise for serious meat-lovers, with beef, veal and duck grilled to perfection over an open fire. The wine list is pretty good too.

✉ **Carrer de les Hortes 16** ☎ **972 22 31 61** 🕐 **Lunch and dinner. Closed Sun**

Boira (££)

Tapas downstairs and a smart restaurant upstairs, featuring modern, light versions of traditional Catalan cuisine. Get here early for one of the tables overlooking the river.

✉ **Plaça Independència 17** ☎ **972 20 30 96** 🕐 **Lunch and dinner daily**

Café Mozart (££)

This popular restaurant serves delicious pizzas, cooked in a wood-fired oven, as well as fondues and grilled meat dishes; there is a wide range of salads.

✉ **Plaça Independència 2** ☎ **972 20 75 42** 🕐 **Lunch and dinner. Closed Tue**

Cal Ros (££)

Cal Ros specialises in Catalan classics with an emphasis on meat dishes: pig's feet with garlic mayonnaise, *botifarra* with broad beans. Try the aubergine lasagne with smoked salmon.

✉ **Carrer Cort Reial 9** ☎ **972 21 73 79** 🕐 **Lunch and dinner. Closed Mon**

Casa Marieta (££)

This popular old standby serves traditional Catalan food, such as rabbit, snails, and seafood with garlic mayonnaise, in agreeably old-fashioned surroundings on an arcaded square.

✉ **Plaça Independència 5** ☎ **972 20 10 16** 🕐 **Lunch and dinner. Closed Mon**

El Celler de Can Roca (£££)

Top of the range Catalan cuisine prepared under the guidance of the Roca brothers. The seasonal *menú degustació* includes five dishes, two desserts and a glass of *cava*. Unfortunately it is some way out of town, so take a taxi.

✉ **Carretera Taialà 40** ☎ **972 22 21 57** 🕐 **Lunch and dinner, Closed Mon. Closed first two weeks in Jul**

Cipresaia (££)

An elegant restaurant in the old town, with impeccable service and comfortable sofas around the tables. The food is mainly classic Empordan cuisine.

✉ **Carrer General Fournàs 2**
☎ **972 22 24 49** 🕐 **Lunch and dinner daily**

Creperie Bretonne (££)

Delicious, authentic French pancakes and cider from Brittany in fashionable and unusual surroundings. Among the idiosyncracies, one table is placed inside an old bus.

✉ **Carrer Cort Reial 14**
☎ **972 21 81 20** 🕐 **Lunch and dinner. Closed Sun. Closed Mon in winter**

Detapes (£)

On a busy road near the station, but the best selection of *tapas* in Girona. Come here for a snack and a beer before catching your train.

✉ **Carretera de Barcelona 13**
☎ **972 41 01 64** 🕐 **Lunch and dinner daily**

La Llibreria (£)

Trendy student café attached to a radical bookshop, serving breakfasts, omelettes, snacks and good value set meals.

✉ **Carrer Cintadans 15** ☎ **972 20 48 18** 🕐 **10–2, 5–9. Closed Sun**

La Marina (££)

Seafood restaurant with tables overlooking the river. Unusual *mar i muntanya* dishes and a *sarsuela* fish casserole.

✉ **Plaça Independència 14**
☎ **972 21 36 57** 🕐 **Lunch and dinner. Closed Tue**

Mar Plaça (£££)

An up-market fish restaurant specialising in fish soups and casseroles as well as simply grilled fresh fish.

✉ **Plaça Independència 3**
☎ **972 20 59 62** 🕐 **Lunch and dinner daily**

El Museu del Vi (£)

Cellar bar specialising in the usual range of *tapas* and good Catalan home cooking, with a good range of local wines.

✉ **Carrer Cort Reial 4** ☎ **972 21 34 85** 🕐 **9AM–2AM. Closed Mon**

El Pati Verd (£££)

This restaurant is inside the Hotel Carlemany. It has a *menú degustació* which changes weekly. Specialities include reliable Catalan favourites such as slow-cooked veal and rabbit with snails.

✉ **Plaça Miquel Santaló 1**
☎ **972 21 12 12** 🕐 **Lunch and dinner. Closed Sun eve**

El Pou del Call (££)

For good-value Catalan cuisine with an excellent *menú del día*. And, as this is in Girona's Jewish quarter, they also serve kosher wines imported from Israel.

✉ **Carrer de la Força 14**
☎ **972 22 37 74** 🕐 **Lunch and dinner. Closed Sun eve**

La Taverna (£)

Tapas, omelettes, local sausages and cheeses, as well as home-made patés and Basque cider, are the favourites here, all served at outdoor tables on a pleasant, square, free from the noise of traffic.

✉ **Plaça Mercadal 2**
🕐 **Open all day, Mon–Sat**

Opening Times

The Spanish like to eat late – typically between 1 and 3 at lunchtime and any time after 9 in the evening. If you get hungry before these times, *tapas* bars are usually open all day. Most restaurants close for one day a week and many have an annual holiday or reduce their hours in winter, so it is always a good idea to telephone in advance.

Central Costa Brava

Set Menus

Most restaurants offer a *menú del día* at lunchtime, and some in the evening, too – a set-price three-course meal, with mineral water or wine included. You may not get much choice (typically two or three options for each course), but what you do get will invariably be cheap, filling and freshly cooked. A full meal, with drinks, will usually cost about the same as a main course from the *carta*.

Aiguablava
Aigua Blava (£££)
This delightful family-run hotel has one of the best restaurants on the Costa Brava, with delicious Catalan specialities like roast turbot and chicken with lobster.
✉ Platja de Fornells ☎ 972 62 20 58 🕔 Lunch and dinner daily, Mar–Oct

Besalú
Ca'n Quei (£)
Good-value bar on a quiet square, serving snacks, sandwiches, salads and hot meals.
✉ Plaça Sant Vicenç ☎ 972 59 00 85 🕔 Lunch and dinner, Thu–Tue

Curia Reial (££)
This restaurant in the 14th-century Royal Court building specialises in Catalan meat and game dishes. There is a terrace overlooking the river and the medieval bridge.
✉ Plaça Llibertat ☎ 972 59 02 63 🕔 Lunch and dinner. Closed Mon eve and Tue

Els Fogons de Can Llaudes (£££)
This elegant restaurant is housed in a Romanesque chapel facing the church of Sant Pere. The emphasis is on meat and game dishes, such as venison, wild boar and roast lamb.
✉ Prat de Sant Pere 4 ☎ 972 59 08 58 🕔 Lunch and dinner. Closed Tue

Calella de Palafrugell
Can Pep (££)
Fish stews are the speciality at this rustic Catalan restaurant, in a delightful village house covered in bougainvillaea.
✉ Carrer Lladó 22 ☎ 972 61 50 00 🕔 Lunch and dinner. Closed Wed

La Gavina (££)
Fresh fish dishes changing daily and charcoal-grilled meats on a vine-covered terrace, just off the main square.
✉ Carrer de la Gravina 7 ☎ 972 61 45 54 🕔 Lunch and dinner daily

El Sot (££)
The people of Palafrugell head for Calella at weekend lunchtimes and this seafood restaurant on the beach is one of the most popular.
✉ Platja del Canadell ☎ 972 61 57 20 🕔 Lunch and dinner daily, Jun–Sep

L'Estartit
La Gaviota (£££)
This seafood restaurant at the end of the promenade has a good view of the Medes islands. Among the meat dishes are unusual items such as ostrich in celery sauce.
✉ Passeig Marítim 92 ☎ 972 75 20 19 🕔 Lunch Tue–Sun, dinner Tue–Sat

Llafranc
La Txata (££)
The interesting sculptures decorating this Basque restaurant were done by Yolanda Uriarte, who looks after the customers while her sister, Itziar, rustles up inventive versions of Basque and Catalan meat and seafood dishes. The overall effect is both stylish and charming.
✉ Carrer Carndo 12 ☎ 972 30 28 78 🕔 Lunch and dinner daily in summer. Fri–Sun in winter

Olot
La Deu (££)
The famous Garrotxa potato dish *patates de la Deu* was invented at this traditional Catalan restaurant.

✉ **Carretera La Deu** ☎ **972 26 10 04** 🕐 **Lunch daily, dinner Mon–Sat**

Palafrugell
Mas Oliver (££)
Country cooking in a large house situated on the edge of town.

✉ **Avinguda d'Espanya 68** ☎ **972 30 10 41** 🕐 **Lunch and dinner. Closed Tue**

La Xicra (£££)
Classic Empordan cooking in a village house. The specialities include seafood casserole and chickpeas with baby octopus and ham.

✉ **Carrer de Sant Antoni 17** ☎ **972 30 56 30** 🕐 **Lunch Thu–Tue, dinner Thu–Mon**

Pals
Mas de Torrent (£££)
Innovative meat and fish dishes prepared with typical Catalan flair, in a beautiful 18th-century farmhouse.

✉ **Torrent, between Pals and Palafrugell** ☎ **972 30 32 92** 🕐 **Lunch and dinner daily**

Sa Punta (£££)
Fresh Empordan produce, simply presented, in this fine Catalan restaurant with delightful gardens.

✉ **Platja de Pals** ☎ **972 63 64 10** 🕐 **Lunch and dinner daily. Closed mid-Jan to mid-Feb**

Peratallada
Can Bonay (££)
The chef in this third-generation family restaurant produces Catalan classics like goose with turnips and partridge wrapped in cabbage. Diners can also explore the wine cellar.

✉ **Plaça de les Voltes 13** ☎ **972 63 40 34** 🕐 **Lunch daily, dinner Fri and Sat**

Can Nau (££)
Hearty Catalan casseroles, of snails, rabbit or chicken, served in the ground floor of a village home.

✉ **Carrer Jaume II 1** ☎ **972 63 40 35** 🕐 **Lunch and dinner, Thu–Tue**

La Riera (££)
Simple Catalan cooking – grilled meat, sausages, snails – at this hotel on the main square.

✉ **Plaça de les Voltes 3** ☎ **972 63 41 42** 🕐 **Lunch and dinner. Closed Tue**

Púbol
Can Bosch (£)
Traditional village restaurant serving hearty portions and a good value set lunch.

✉ **Beside the castle** ☎ **972 48 83 57** 🕐 **Lunch daily, dinner Thu–Sat**

Santa Pau
Cal Sastre (££)
The cuisine of the Garrotxa, featuring local sausages, mushrooms and beans, served underneath the arches on a delightful square.

✉ **Placeta dels Balls 6** ☎ **972 68 04 21** 🕐 **Lunch, Tue–Sun**

Tamariu
Es Dofí (££)
One of the best of the many fish restaurants along the seafront promenade.

✉ **Passeig del Mar 22** ☎ **972 62 00 43** 🕐 **Lunch and dinner daily**

Tapas
Tapas are a Spanish institution. Originally a free 'lid' (*tapa*) of ham placed across a drink, nowadays they consist of small portions of everything from octopus to olives. Locals tend to snack on *tapas* during the day before going home for dinner, but several portions can make a filling meal in itself. Popular *tapas* include stuffed peppers, fried squid rings and plates of cured ham. And you don't have to look at a menu – just point to what you want in the cabinet beneath the bar.

The North Coast & Beyond

Vegetarians

Vegetarians could have a hard time in the Costa Brava – unless they are prepared to eat fish. *Tapas* bars usually have vegetarian options, including a range of omelettes; or you could have a plate of *pa amb tomàquet* (bread rubbed with tomato) accompanied by a large Catalan salad without the meat. Unfortunately, many vegetable dishes include small pieces of meat or fish, but you can always try asking for it *sense carn* (without meat).

Cadaqués

Casa Anita (£)

At Casa Anita the simple, rustic home cooking is served at communal wooden tables. The authentic atmosphere is a popular choice for locals and tourists alike.

✉ **Carrer Miquel Rosset 16**
☎ **972 25 84 71** 🕔 **Lunch and dinner daily**

La Galiota (££)

Oven-baked fish is the house speciality at this sophisticated Catalan restaurant near the village museum.

✉ **Carrer Narcis Monturiol 9**
☎ **972 25 81 87** 🕔 **Lunch and dinner daily May–Sep**

El Pescador (££)

An evocatively located harbourside fish restaurant with outdoor tables facing the beach.

✉ **Carrer Nemesi Llorens**
☎ **972 25 88 59** 🕔 **Lunch and dinner. Closed Thu**

Castelló d'Empúries

Canet (££)

A range of local meat dishes as well as highly welcome vegetarian and children's menus are available in this restaurant in a friendly hotel in the centre of town.

✉ **Plaça Joc de la Pilota 2**
☎ **972 25 03 40** 🕔 **Lunch and dinner. Closed Mon**

Empúries

Mesón del Conde (££)

The best of the restaurants in the village of Sant Martí d'Empúries is just a short walk from the ruins. In spring try grilled *calçots*, a local onion served with *romesco* sauce.

✉ **Plaça Major, Sant Martí d'Empúries** ☎ **972 77 03 06**
🕔 **Lunch and dinner daily**

L'Escala

Els Pescadors (£££)

Traditional Catalan cooking using top-quality local ingredients – grilled fish, marinated partridge and *sarsuela* fish casserole. A good place for a celebration.

✉ **Carrer Port d'en Perris 3**
☎ **972 77 07 28** 🕔 **Lunch and dinner daily. Closed Nov**

El Roser 2 (£££)

Fresh fish and seafood with wonderful views over the Gulf of Roses.

✉ **Passeig Lluís Albert 1**
☎ **972 77 11 02** 🕔 **Lunch and dinner daily. Closed Feb**

Figueres

Ampurdán (£££)

This famous hotel, just outside Figueres on the old road to France, has a magnificent garden terrace, where traditional Empordan cooking is served up with modern flair. The former chef here, Josep Mercader, is considered to be the founder of modern Catalan cuisine.

✉ **Antiga Carretera de França**
☎ **972 50 05 62** 🕔 **Lunch and dinner daily**

Antaviana (££)

Stylish Catalan and French cuisine with an emphasis on duck – try the *carpaccio* of duck breast or the beef in Cabrales (blue cheese) sauce.

✉ **Carrer Llers 5** ☎ **972 51 03 77** 🕔 **Lunch Mon–Sat, dinner Mon and Wed–Sat**

Dalícatessen

This trendy sandwich and salad bar is a good place for a snack before or after a visit to the Dalí museum.

✉ **Carrer Sant Pere 19** ☎ **972 50 41 76** 🕔 **8AM–9PM daily**

El Dragon Dorado (£)

If you've had enough of Catalan cooking, try this Cantonese restaurant near the Dalí museum.

✉ **Pujada del Castell 9** ☎ **972 50 04 17** 🕐 **Lunch and dinner daily**

Durán (££)

Salvador Dalí's favourite hangout is still full of character, and continues to serve good local food in a traditional Catalan style.

✉ **Carrer Lasauca 5** ☎ **972 50 12 50** 🕐 **Lunch and dinner daily**

El Setrill d'Or (£)

For good pizzas and fresh pasta dishes, and an excellent-value set lunch. The comfortable furnishings and oil paintings on the walls add to the atmosphere.

✉ **Carrer Tortellà 12** ☎ **972 50 55 40** 🕐 **Lunch and dinner daily. Closed Mon and Tue in winter**

Llançà

La Brasa (££)

Local squid and anchovies, seafood casserole and charcoal-grilled meat, served on a pretty terrace just back from the harbour.

✉ **Plaça Catalunya 6** ☎ **972 38 02 02** 🕐 **Lunch and dinner daily. Closed Tue. Closed Dec–Mar**

Can Manel (££)

Great seafood dishes and overlooking the harbour – lobster *flambée*, local mussels and crustaceans, monkfish with almonds, home-smoked fish are notable highlights.

✉ **Passeig Marítim** ☎ **972 38 01 12** 🕐 **Lunch and dinner daily. Closed Thu**

Peralada

Ca La Maria (££)

The setting of this restaurant is delightful, in an 18th-century inn with stone arcades. The food is classic country cooking, with dishes such as roast kid, plus game and wild mushrooms in season.

✉ **Carrer Unió 5, Mollet de Peralada** ☎ **972 56 33 82** 🕐 **Lunch and dinner Wed–Mon**

Portbou

L'Áncora (££)

Good-value fish restaurant on the promenade facing the beach, designed to catch the French day-trippers before they get back on the train.

✉ **Passeig de la Sardana** ☎ **972 39 00 25** 🕐 **Lunch and dinner. Closed Tues**

Roses

El Bulli (£££)

Quite simply one of the finest restaurants in Spain (▶ panel). Book ahead.

✉ **Cala Montjoi** ☎ **972 15 04 57** 🕐 **Lunch and dinner daily Jul–Sep**

Flor de Lis (£££)

Sophisticated French and seafood cuisine in a pretty cottage in the back streets.

✉ **Carrer Coscanilles 47** ☎ **972 25 43 16** 🕐 **Dinner only, Wed–Mon**

La Llar (£££)

Creative Catalan meat and fish dishes in a delightfully restored farmhouse just outside the town. If you're feeling adventurous go for the 'surprise menu'.

✉ **Carretera Figueres km4** ☎ **972 25 53 68** 🕐 **Lunch and dinner daily. Closed Wed eve and Thu in winter**

El Bulli

People travel from all over Catalonia to eat at this famous restaurant, in an exceptional setting looking down over a tranquil cove. The chef, Ferràn Adrià, has recently gained his third Michelin star for his highly personal Catalan cuisine and signature dishes, such as bone marrow with caviar. Expect to pay around 15,000 ptas per person; if you really want to do it in style, arrive by boat.

The South Coast & Beyond

Wine

Catalonia produces some excellent wines (► 73), but the best wines on the menu will probably come from La Rioja. Riojan reds, made with the *tempranillo* grape, are superb. Those labelled *crianza* are aged in oak; *reserva* and *gran reserva* have been aged for longer. Don't forget *cava*, Catalan sparkling wine, which is such good value that you don't even need a special excuse to drink it.

Blanes
Can Flores (££)
Fresh seafood dishes and varied international cuisine at this harbourside restaurant near the fishing port.

✉ **Esplanada del Port** ☎ **972 33 00 07** 🕐 **Lunch and dinner daily**

El Port (££)
Come here to eat freshly caught fish beneath the harbour walls. The lobster and sea bass are expensive but there is a very affordable set lunch, which features paella or mussels and fresh fish.

✉ **Esplanada del Port** ☎ **972 33 48 19** 🕐 **Lunch and dinner daily**

El Ventall (£££)
One of the top restaurants in this area is found in a country house between Blanes and Lloret de Mar. The cooking is Mediterranean and modern Catalan, and in summer you can eat outside on a garden terrace.

✉ **Carretera de Lloret km2** ☎ **972 33 29 81** 🕐 **Lunch Wed–Mon, dinner Wed–Sun**

Lloret de Mar
El Trull (£££)
This popular fish restaurant overlooking a pretty cove has a terrace with a pool in summer. Choose your own lobster then watch it being grilled.

✉ **Cala Canyelles** ☎ **972 36 49 28** 🕐 **Lunch and dinner daily**

Palamós
La Gamba (£££)
The best local seafood, simply prepared, on a terrace overlooking the harbour.

Specialities are prawns, *suquet* casserole (► 72), oven-baked fish and stuffed sea urchins.

✉ **Plaça Sant Pere 1** ☎ **972 31 46 33** 🕐 **Lunch and dinner, Thu–Tue**

Maria de Cadaqués (£££)
Trendy fish restaurant which displays paintings by local artists on the walls. Fish comes fresh from the local fleet to become delicious *suquets*.

✉ **Carrer Tauler i Servià 6** ☎ **972 31 40 09** 🕐 **Lunch Tue–Sun, dinner Tue–Sat. Closed mid-Dec to Jan**

Platja d'Aro
Big Rock (£££)
Carles Camós' restaurant, in an old mansion above the town, has become known for its inventive modern Catalan cuisine. Try the lobster casserole or the sea bass cooked in *cava*.

✉ **Avinguda Barri de Fanals** ☎ **972 81 80 12** 🕐 **Lunch Tue–Sun, dinner Tue–Sat**

El Cau del Pernil (££)
This traditional cellar-bar specialises in ham, as well as several varieties of sausages and charcoal-grilled meat. A meat eater's heaven.

✉ **Avinguda Sant Feliu 7** ☎ **972 81 72 09** 🕐 **Lunch and dinner daily**

Fanals Platja (££–£££)
Seafood restaurant looking out on to the beach. The specialities, including lobster paella, are expensive, but you don't have to spend a fortune here.

✉ **Passeig Marítim 92** ☎ **972 81 98 26** 🕐 **Lunch and dinner daily**

Hipopotamus (££)
Simple Spanish and Catalan classics served at bustling outdoor tables on the main street.
✉ Avinguda S'Agaró 53 ☎ 972 81 77 60 🕐 Lunch and dinner daily

Sant Feliu de Guíxols
Bahía (££)
Popular fish restaurant on the promenade. Start with a *pica-pica*, a selection of a dozen fishy *tapas*.
✉ Passeig del Mar 17 ☎ 972 32 02 19 🕐 Lunch and dinner daily

Can Salvi (££)
The emphasis here is on locally caught fish, including anchovies, salmon and sole in Roquefort sauce.
✉ Passeig del Mar 23 ☎ 972 32 10 13 🕐 Lunch and dinner, Thu–Tue. Closed mid-Nov to mid-Dec

Can Toni (££)
Back-street bar serving exquisite fish dishes – stuffed anchovies, *suquet* casserole and chicken with prawns.
✉ Carrer Nou del Garrofer 54 ☎ 972 32 10 26 🕐 Lunch and dinner daily

El Dorado Petit (£££)
Catalan cuisine based on fresh seasonal produce with French and Italian influences. The same owners have a cheaper grill-bar next door.
✉ Rambla Vidal 23 ☎ 972 32 18 18 🕐 Lunch and dinner, Thu–Tue

Naùtic (££)
Seafood, rice and *mar i muntanya* dishes (► 72), looking out across the fishing boats in the harbour.
✉ Es Port ☎ 972 32 06 63 🕐 Lunch Tue–Sun, dinner Tue–Sat

Tossa de Mar
Bahía (££)
This is the best place to eat fresh fish on the seafront.
✉ Passeig del Mar 19 ☎ 972 34 03 22 🕐 Lunch and dinner. Closed Wed

Es Molí (££)
Regional meat and fish dishes served in an attractive and unusual setting – the garden of an old windmill, surrounded by arcades.
✉ Carrer Tarull 5 ☎ 972 34 14 14 🕐 Lunch and dinner, Wed–Mon. Closed in winter

Vic
Café Nou (£)
Noisy, bustling locals' pub, which gets packed out on market days. The set menu here is one of the best deals anywhere.
✉ Plaça Major 23 ☎ 938 86 25 02 🕐 Lunch and dinner, Tue–Sun

El Jardinet (££)
Catalan cooking with a hint of French in a delightful restaurant in the back streets of the old town.
✉ Carrer dels Corretgers 6 ☎ 938 86 28 77 🕐 Lunch Tue–Sun, dinner Tue–Sat

La Taula (££)
A wide assortment of *tapas*, as well as main meals, served in an old mansion in the medieval centre.
✉ Plaça Don Miquel de Clariana 4 ☎ 938 86 32 29 🕐 Lunch Tue–Sun, dinner Tue–Sat

Coffee
In Spain, *un café* after your meal means only one thing – *café solo* (*café sol* in Catalan), which is short, strong and black, like an espresso. If you want hot milk added, ask for *café con leche* or *café amb llet*. If the waiter brings you a brandy or a liqueur with your coffee, this is a treat on the house. Drink up and enjoy!

Girona & Central Costa Brava

Prices
Prices are approximate, based on a double room in summer, without breakfast or 7 per cent VAT:

£ = under 10,000 ptas
££ = 10,000–20,000 ptas
£££ = over 20,000 ptas

You can usually get a single room for around 60 per cent of the cost of a double. Hotel prices often vary between seasons and will always be much lower than the published rates if booked as part of a package holiday.

Aiguablava
Aigua Blava (££)
One of the gems of the Catalan coast, with a succession of white-painted buildings tumbling down towards a rocky cove. Many rooms are in bungalows in the gardens, which also contain tennis courts and a pool. It was recently rewarded with the accolade of Europe's most family-friendly hotel.
✉ Platja de Fornells ☎ 972 62 20 58 🕐 Mid-Feb to Nov

Parador de Aiguablava (£££)
A member of the state-run chain of *paradors*, set amid delightful pine groves. Steps down to the beach and good views of the bay.
✉ Platja d'Aiguablava ☎ 972 62 21 62 🕐 All year

Besalú
Fonda Siqués (£)
An old stone-built inn on the main road through the town, with a dining-room based in the old stables.
✉ Avinguda President Lluís Companys 6 ☎ 972 59 01 10 🕐 Closed Dec

Calella de Palafrugell
Sant Roc (££)
Traditional seaside hotel on a spectacular position on a rocky outcrop looking down over the bay. There are steps from the hotel to the beach.
✉ Plaça de l'Atlàntic 2 ☎ 972 61 42 50 🕐 Mar–Oct

La Torre (£)
Simple hotel with a terrace overlooking the bay between Calella and Llafranc.
✉ Passeig de la Torre 28 ☎ 972 61 46 03 🕐 Jun–Sep

L'Estartit
Panorama (£)
The Panorama is the biggest and the best of all the family hotels along the seafront in L'Estartit and has its own swimming pool.
✉ Avinguda de Grècia 5 ☎ 972 75 10 92 🕐 Apr–Oct

Girona
Bellmirall (£)
This is the best place to stay if you are more interested in characterful than luxurious accommodation – the Bellmirall is a medieval stone mansion in the old town which has been turned into a charming hostel with simple but comfortable rooms overlooking the cathedral.
✉ Carrer Bellmirall 3 ☎ 972 20 40 09 🕐 Mar–Dec

Carlemany (££)
A smart and modern hotel with excellent restaurant facilities, the Carlemany is only a few minutes' walk from the medieval centre of the city.
✉ Plaça Miquel Santaló 1 ☎ 972 21 12 12 🕐 All year

Costabella (££)
Modern hotel on the road out of town towards Figueres. Conveniently helps you avoid the problem of finding somewhere to park in the city centre.
✉ Avinguda de França 61 ☎ 972 20 25 24 🕐 All year

Melià Confort Girona (££)
A large hotel, particularly popular with business people, on the outskirts of the city, near the railway station.
✉ Carretera de Barcelona 112 ☎ 972 40 05 00 🕐 All year

Peninsula (£)

A comfortable hotel in an excellent central location, on a pedestrianised street beside the Pont de Pedra and close to Girona's old town.

✉ **Carrer Nou 3**
☎ **972 20 38 00** 🕐 **All year**

Ultonia (££)

This smart but functional hotel is on a busy road in the new town. Handy for outings but a little noisy.

✉ **Gran Via de Jaume I 22**
☎ **972 20 38 50** 🕐 **All year**

Llafranc
Llafranch (££)

A stylish and comfortable hotel on the seafront promenade in Llafranc, with a considerable reputation for good food. This was one of the first tourist hotels on the Costa Brava and is still run by the same family. Salvador Dalí was a regular visitor and the bar is lined with pictures of Dalí with flamenco dancers, singers and the brothers who ran the hotel at that time.

✉ **Passeig de Cípsela 16**
☎ **972 30 02 08** 🕐 **All year**

Llevant (££)

A small, attractive hotel with a pleasantly situated restaurant, on a terrace overlooking the sea.

✉ **Carrer Francesc de Blanes 5**
☎ **972 30 03 66** 🕐 **All year**

Olot
Riu Olot (££)

This comfortable four-star hotel on the edge of the town would make a good base for excursions into the Garrotxa Natural Park.

✉ **Carretera Santa Pau**
☎ **972 26 94 44** 🕐 **All year**

Palafrugell
Plaja (£)

Simple *pension* in the centre, with rooms arranged around an attractive courtyard.

✉ **Carrer Sant Sebastià 34**
☎ **972 61 08 28** 🕐 **All year**

Pals
La Costa (£££)

Luxury modern hotel situated beside a golf course, with facilities including tennis courts, a gym and a children's pool.

✉ **Urbanització Arenals de Mar** ☎ **972 66 77 40**
🕐 **Feb–Oct**

Mas de Torrent (£££)

An 18th-century farmhouse, with period furniture, contemporary Catalan art and flower-filled gardens. One of the finest hotels in the region, known for its innovative Catalan cuisine.

✉ **Torrent, between Pals and Palafrugell** ☎ **972 30 32 92**
🕐 **All year**

Santa Pau
Cal Sastre (££)

Run by the owners of Santa Pau's best restaurant, in an old farmhouse just outside the town walls. A good base for a walking holiday.

✉ **Carrer de les Cases Noves 1**
☎ **972 68 00 49** 🕐 **All year**

Tamariu
Hostalillo (££)

Three-star hotel overlooking the beach.

✉ **Carrer Bellavista 22**
☎ **972 620228** 🕐 **Apr–Sep**

Tamariu (£)

A small and friendly hotel – well situated, right beside the beach.

✉ **Passeig del Mar 2** ☎ **972 62 00 31** 🕐 **May to mid-Nov**

Hotels, *Pensions* and *Paradors*

All tourist accommodation in Catalonia is strictly classified and graded by the government. Hotels are graded from one to five stars according to facilities; *pensions*, with fewer facilities but sometimes just as comfortable, are graded either one or two. *Pensions* will not necessarily offer rooms with private bathrooms. *Paradors* are luxury, state-run hotels, mostly in historic buildings or areas of scenic beauty. The only two *paradors* in the Costa Brava region are at Aiguablava and Vic.

The North Coast & Beyond

Apartments

A week in a self-catering apartment or villa can work out a lot cheaper than staying in a hotel. Most can only be booked through tour operators, but a few are advertised individually by their owners or available for rent through local agencies in the Costa Brava. Some apartments have their own private pools. If you want an apartment in summer it is essential to book several months in advance.

Cadaqués

Blaumar (££)

A pleasant looking, two-star hotel only 200m from the beach and less than 500m from the centre of town, the Blauma boasts the usual facilities including pool and sun terrace.

✉ Carrer Massa d'Or 21 ☎ 972 15 90 20/972 15 90 41, fax 972 15 93 36 🕔 Jan, Mar–Oct, Dec

Playa Sol (££)

Old-fashioned seaside hotel with a swimming pool in the gardens and a small beach decked out with fishing boats directly opposite.

✉ Platja Pianc 3 ☎ 972 25 81 00 🕔 All year

La Residència (££)

Stylish *Modernista* hotel on the seafront, with a sundial by Dalí and an art gallery.

✉ Caritat Serinyana 1 ☎ 972 25 83 12 🕔 All year

Rocamar (££)

Traditional seaside hotel with a sea water pool and steps down to a rocky cove.

✉ Carrer Verge del Carme ☎ 972 25 81 50 🕔 All year

S'Aguarda (£)

Family-run hotel with a rooftop terrace. All of the rooms have sea views.

✉ Carretera Portlligat 28 ☎ 972 25 80 82 🕔 All year

Castelló d'Empúries

Allioli (£)

This restored 17th-century farmhouse, just off the main Roses to Figueres road, has wooden beams in the bedrooms and a popular, traditional restaurant.

✉ Urbanització Castell Nou ☎ 972 25 03 00 🕔 Mar–Dec

Canet (£)

Delightful town-centre hotel with a swimming pool in its interior courtyard.

✉ Plaça Joc de la Pilota 2 ☎ 972 25 03 40 🕔 Dec–Oct

Colera

La Gambina (£)

A comfortable, two-star beach hotel; most of the rooms have balconies facing the sea.

✉ Passeig del Mar ☎ 972 38 91 72 🕔 Apr–Dec

Empúries

Ampurias (£)

Simple and peaceful beach *pension*, near the Greek and Roman ruins.

✉ Afores ☎ 972 77 02 07 🕔 Jun–Sep

L'Escala

Nieves Mar (£)

Smart, three-star hotel on the promenade, with a swimming pool and tennis courts in the garden.

✉ Passeig Marítim 8 ☎ 972 77 03 00 🕔 Apr–Oct

Figueres

Ampurdán (££)

This stylish hotel, just north of Figueres, was the birthplace of the new Catalan cuisine and is still an essential place of pilgrimage for food-lovers.

✉ Antiga Carretera de França (N11) ☎ 972 50 05 62 🕔 All year

Durán (££)

An atmospheric, old-world hotel in the centre of town, where Salvador Dalí used to meet his friends for lunch. It also has one of the finest restaurants in Figueres.

✉ Carrer Lasauca 5 ☎ 972 50 12 50 🕔 All year

España (£)
An inexpensive and centrally located pension, close to the Dalí museum. Rooms can be with or without bath and there is a good-value restaurant on the ground floor.

✉ **Carrer La Jonquera 26**
☎ **972 50 08 69** 🕐 **All year**

President (£)
Comfortable, three-star hotel with private parking on the ring road close to the centre of town.

✉ **Ronda Firal 33** ☎ **972 50 17 00** 🕐 **All year**

Llançà
Berna (£)
Old-fashioned seaside hotel with great views over the harbour.

✉ **Passeig Marítim 13** ☎ **972 38 01 50** 🕐 **Jun–Sep**

Grimar (£)
The top hotel in the resort, 2km from the beach but with a swimming pool and landscaped gardens looking out to sea.

✉ **Carretera de Portbou**
☎ **972 38 01 67** 🕐 **Apr–Oct**

El Port de la Selva
Porto Cristo (£)
A fairly comfortable, two-star hotel in the village centre, just a short way back from the sea.

✉ **Carrer Major 59** ☎ **972 38 70 62** 🕐 **Apr–Oct**

Portlligat
Calina (££)
This apartment style hotel, close to the beach, has a series of self-catering apartments set around a swimming pool.

✉ **Portlligat** ☎ **972 25 88 51**
🕐 **Apr–Sep**

Portlligat (££)
A peaceful, two-star hotel with a children's playground, a swimming pool and views over Dalí's house and out to sea.

✉ **Portlligat** ☎ **972 25 81 62**
🕐 **All year**

Roses
Almadraba Park (££)
Four-star hotel with modern facilities, on a rocky cliff overlooking the cove of Almadrava.

✉ **Platja de Almadrava**
☎ **972 25 65 50** 🕐 **Apr–Oct**

Canyelles Platja (££)
The Canyelles Platja is a typical seaside hotel with a swimming pool and facing the Canyelles beach, to the southeast of the town.

✉ **Platja Canyelles** ☎ **972 25 65 00** 🕐 **Jun–Sep**

Marítim (£)
Good-value, two-star hotel on the seafront, with one pool for adults and another for kids.

✉ **Platja Salatar** ☎ **972 25 63 90** 🕐 **Mar–Dec**

La Terraza (££)
This modern, four-star hotel faces directly on to the beach and is only 300m from the bustling centre of town.

✉ **Avinguda de Rhode 30**
☎ **972 25 61 54** 🕐 **Apr–Oct**

Vistabella (££)
This three-star hotel, beside the beach at Canyelles, has its own landing-stage for boats and a variety of spa-like health treatments, ranging from massage to Turkish baths.

✉ **Cala Canyelles Petites**
☎ **972 25 62 00** 🕐 **All year**

Agrotourism
A number of farmers in the region let out rooms in their houses or in restored farm buildings on their land, on a self-catering, bed-and-breakfast or full-board basis. This can be a great way of getting to meet a local family and enjoying an active holiday away from the beach resorts. A brochure on rural tourism in the Costa Brava is available from Turisme Rural Girona ☎ 972 22 60 15.

The South Coast

Spa Hotels

The waters of the Selva region, south of Girona, have long been known for their healing properties. Caldes de Malavella, a Roman spa town (▶ 78), has two elegant spa hotels, built around the turn of the century in neo-classical and Modernist styles: Balneari Prats ☎ 972 47 00 51 and Vichy Catalán ☎ 972 47 00 00. Termes Orión ☎ 972 84 00 65 is another spa-hotel in the nearby town of Santa Coloma de Farners.

Calonge
Park Hotel San Jorge (££)
Four-star hotel overlooking a rugged stretch of coastline, with access on foot to a pair of secluded coves.
✉ Carretera de Palamós ☎ 972 65 23 11 🕐 All year

Rey Mar (£)
Three-star hotel on the edge of a pretty bay, with swimming pool, tennis courts and marvellous sea views.
✉ Torre Valentina ☎ 972 65 22 11 🕐 Jun–Sep

Lloret de Mar
Gran Hotel Monterrey (££)
Luxury hotel on the outskirts of the resort, with a swimming pool and tennis courts in its extensive grounds.
✉ Carretera Blanes-Tossa de Mar ☎ 972 36 40 50 🕐 Apr–Oct

Santa Marta (£££)
Smart, modern hotel set in a pine wood behind the quiet cove of Santa Cristina, with acres of flower gardens and stunning sea views.
✉ Platja Santa Cristina ☎ 972 36 49 04 🕐 Feb–Dec

Palamós
La Fosca (£)
Modest but comfortable two-star *pension*, set back from the beach in its own quiet bay.
✉ Passeig de la Fosca 24 ☎ 972 60 10 71 🕐 All year

Trias (££)
Luxury and elegance go hand in hand in this modern beach hotel, with a range of facilities including a swimming pool and a solarium.
✉ Passeig del Mar ☎ 972 60 18 00 🕐 Apr–Sep

Platja d'Aro
Big Rock (£££)
This mansion high above the town is better known as one of the best restaurants on the Costa Brava, but if you want to stay after your meal there are five luxury suites upstairs and a swimming pool in the beautifully landscaped gardens.
✉ Carrer Barri de Fanals 5 ☎ 972 81 80 12 🕐 All year

Platja Park (££)
Busy, four-star hotel in the centre of town, with a children's pool and play area and a programme of nightly entertainment. The beach is about 10 minutes' walk away.
✉ Avinguda de Strasburg 10 ☎ 972 81 68 05 🕐 Mar–Dec

Xaloc (££)
A comfortable, three-star hotel, with a quiet terrace garden leading to the small beach of Platja Rovira.
✉ Cala Rovira ☎ 972 81 73 00 🕐 Apr–Sep

S'Agaró
Hostal de la Gavina (£££)
The most famous hotel on the Costa Brava was opened in 1924 and designed by the Catalan Modernist architect Rafael Masó in the style of a Gothic villa. Film stars such as Orson Welles and Elizabeth Taylor have stayed here, enjoying its antiques, tapestries and marble floors, its fine Catalan cuisine and its landscaped gardens on a rocky promontory above the sea.
✉ Plaça de la Rosaleda ☎ 972 32 11 00 🕐 Mar–Oct

S'Agaró (££)

Less exclusive than its famous neighbour, this luxury four-star hotel also has its own extensive gardens, just a short walk from the beach.

⊠ Platja Sant Pol ☎ 972 32 52 00 🕒 All year

Sant Feliu de Guíxols
Caleta Park (££)

Four-star hotel, with swimming pool and tennis courts, beside a small beach to the north of the town.

⊠ Platja Sant Pol ☎ 972 32 00 12 🕒 Mar–Nov

Casa Rovira (£)

English-run country house on the outskirts of town, with gardens beneath the pine woods. No pool, just good home cooking and an arty, Bohemian atmosphere for those looking for something different.

☎ Carrer Sant Amanç 106 ☎ 972 32 12 02 🕒 May–Oct

Edén Roc (££)

Large hotel set in its own grounds beside the cove of Port Salvi. The hotel's facilities include a swimming pool and a children's playground.

⊠ Port Salvi ☎ 972 32 01 00 🕒 Feb–Dec

Tossa de Mar
Costa Brava (£)

With 188 rooms, most with balconies, this is a large, modern hotel, close to the centre of town and the beaches. An à la carte restaurant serves the usual variety of international tourist cuisine.

⊠ Av Verge de Montserrat ☎ 972 34 02 24/972 34 01 30, fax 972 34 21 69 🕒 May–Oct

Diana (£)

Attractive seafront villa, built in the Modernist style with arched windows, stained glass and featuring a fireplace by Antoni Gaudí in the lounge.

⊠ Plaça d'Espanya 6 ☎ 972 34 18 86 🕒 All year

Gran Hotel Reymar (£££)

Arguably the smartest hotel in Tossa, with a heated swimming pool and tennis courts and a pleasant garden with lovely views looking down over the Mar Menuda beach.

⊠ Platja Mar Menuda ☎ 972 34 03 12 🕒 May–Oct

Mar Menuda (££)

Peaceful, traditional hotel on the beach of the same name, just around the bay from Tossa's main beach promenade.

⊠ Platja Mar Menuda ☎ 972 34 10 00 🕒 Jan–Oct

Vic
Parador de Vic (££)

This state-run inn was designed in Catalan farmhouse style, and set in a pine grove overlooking a reservoir at the foot of the Montseny mountains. Although this is a modern building, it places the same emphasis as the rest of the *parador* network on local character and the best of regional cuisine. The restaurant serves up hearty Catalan stews and fresh anglerfish with garlic mayonnaise. There are wonderful views of the mountains from the outdoor swimming pool.

⊠ Pantà de Sau, Carrer de Roda de Ter (14km from Vic) ☎ 938 12 23 23 🕒 All year

Camping

The Costa Brava has over 100 official campsites, most of them clustered around the large coastal resorts. Many are situated right beside beaches, and nearly all have swimming pools. Campsites are classified as first, second or third class, according to facilities. An annual guide, available in local bookshops, lists all the campsites; information is also available from local tourist offices. Relax-Naturista is an official nudist campsite near Palafrugell ☎ 972 30 08 18.

Markets

Costa Brava on the Internet

Like many European resort areas, the Costa Brava has not been slow in developing new technology to help the tourist. You can access a wide range of information, including hotel reservations, through the internet. New websites are developing all the time but amongst the more established sites are www.costabrava.org and www.publintur.es.

Girona
Mercat Municipal
This indoor market near the Plaça de Catalunya has stalls selling a wide range of meat, fish and cheeses, fresh fruit and vegetables, and ready-prepared meals. A good place to stock up on provisions for a picnic.

⊠ **Plaça Salvador Espriu**
🕐 **Mon–Sat 7–1:30**

Mercat Semanal
Girona's weekly markets take place on Tuesday and Saturday, when the Passeig de la Devesa, the promenade in front of Devesa Park, is lined with cheap clothes stalls. On Saturdays a flower market is set up on the Rambla, along with stalls selling bric-à-brac, crafts and antiques.

⊠ **Passeig de la Devesa**
🕐 **Tue, Sat all year**

Weekly Markets
Market day in any of the Costa Brava's towns is the best place to meet the locals and soak up the atmosphere of small-town Catalonia. The usual pattern is for fresh fruit, vegetables and flowers to be sold in or around the main square, together with specialist stalls selling meats and cheeses, biscuits and sweets, and dried fruit and nuts. Spreading out from here will be a haphazard arrangement of street stalls selling everything from cheap underwear to household utensils, and from jewellery to tourist souvenirs. It is not the usual custom to haggle over the price. A few larger towns and resorts, like Blanes, Lloret de Mar and Palafrugell, have daily produce markets from Monday to Saturday, but these are the main weekly market days:

Central Costa Brava
Banyoles – Wed
Begur – Wed
Besalú – Tue
La Bisbal – Fri
L'Estartit – Thu
Olot – Mon
Palafrugell – Sun
Ripoll – Sat
Sant Joan de les Abadesses – Sun
Torroella de Montgrí – Mon

The North Coast & Beyond
Figueres – Thu
Cadaqués – Mon
Castelló d'Empúries – Tue
L'Escala – Sun
Llançà – Wed
El Port de la Selva – Fri
Roses – Sun

The South Coast & Beyond
Blanes – Mon
Caldes de Malavella – Tue
Calonge – Thu
Lloret de Mar – Tue
Palamós – Tue
Platja d'Aro – Fri
Sant Feliu de Guíxols – Sun
Tossa de Mar – Thu
Vic – Tue/Sat

Fish Auctions
That the Costa Brava is a working coast is often overlooked, but a visit to a fish auction in one of the Costa Brava's ports can be a memorable experience. Most take place at around 5PM, when the fishing fleet returns. You can see fish auctions on weekday afternoons in Blanes, L'Escala, Palamós and Roses, in the market halls adjoining each of their fishing harbours.

Food & Drink

The old towns of Girona, Figueres, Olot and Vic are full of speciality food shops – butchers, bakers, delicatessens, pâtisseries. The Catalans take great pride in their traditional foods, and even everyday items like bread and cheese are likely to have been produced by master artisans. Good buys include local sausages, Spanish hams and cheeses, olive oil, wine vinegar, Spanish wines and brandies and anchovies from L'Escala. Those with a sweet tooth should look out for *music*, a fruit and nut cake, and *torró*, a honey and nougat sweetmeat.

Girona
J Candela
This shop sells *turrón* (*torró* in Catalan) produced in the family factory, as well as a wide range of unusual sweets.

✉ **Carrer de l'Argenteria 8**
☎ **972 22 09 38**

Gluki
Makers of chocolate since 1880. A feast of chocolate delicacies, from chocolate teddy bears to slabs of plain, dark chocolate.

✉ **Carrer de l'Argenteria 26**
☎ **972 20 19 89**

Joan Puig
This old-world, wood-panelled grocer's shop sells excellent cheeses, cured meats, oils, wine, coffee and spices.

✉ **Rambla de la Llibertat 7**

Central Costa Brava

Besalú
El Rebost del Comtat
A museum of local history and crafts with a cheese and sausage shop attached, where you can taste before you buy.

✉ **Plaça Llibertat 14** ☎ **972 59 03 07**

Castellfollit de la Roca
Cal Enric
This factory shop sells a tempting selection of *galetes*, delicious local biscuits made with butter and almonds.

✉ **Carretera Girona 6** ☎ **972 29 40 44**

Museu d'Embotits
The sausage museum (▶ 44) sells a selection of cured meats from the Sala factory, which has been based in the village for more than 150 years.

✉ **Carretera Girona**

The North Coast & Beyond

Peralada
Cavas del Castillo de Peralada
Wines from the castle cellars, including some fine *cavas* or sparkling wines.

✉ **Plaça del Carme 1** ☎ **972 53 80 11**

The South Coast & Beyond

Vic
Ca'n Vilada
Carrer dels Argenters has several speciality butchers selling the local sausages for which Vic is famous. This shop at the entrance to the lane is one of the best, with home-made patés and salads as well as numerous varieties of sausage.

✉ **Carrer dels Argenters 1**

Opening Hours
Most shops are open from around 9–1 and 5–8 Monday to Friday, and on Saturday mornings, though shops in the main tourist resorts may stay open during the afternoons and on Sundays. Markets are open in the morning, from around 8–1. The smarter clothes and craft shops are busiest in the evenings, when locals combine a spot of window-shopping with their ritual promenade.

Arts & Crafts

Pottery in La Bisbal

The road out of La Bisbal towards Girona is lined with pottery shops, selling everything from mass-produced factory pieces to innovative local designs. Among the best buys are simple earthenware cooking pots, which are both good quality and excellent value. It pays to shop around, but you are not expected to bargain. Most of these shops are open on Saturday and Sunday evenings.

Central Costa Brava

La Bisbal

Antic Bisbal

As well as pottery shops, La Bisbal also has several devoted to antiques and this is the biggest, with branches at boths ends of town.

✉ **Carrer Sis d'Octubre 39 and Carrer l'Aigüeta 176** ☎ **972 64 34 83**

Bambu Bambu

If you can't face looking at any more pottery, this large shop on La Bisbal's 'ceramic street' has a huge collection of basketware.

✉ **Carrer l'Aigüeta 61** ☎ **972 64 23 33**

Bosch

A large pottery emporium selling everyday items like earthenware plates and cooking pots at good prices.

✉ **Carrer l'Aigüeta 47** ☎ **972 64 12 00**

La Botiga

La Botiga is a pottery and gift shop with a few better pieces hidden away among the displays of tourist kitsch.

✉ **Carrer l'Aigüeta 32** ☎ **972 64 18 02**

Cals Americans

Modern reproductions of antique Catalan plates are among the items on display at this arty pottery shop.

✉ **Carrer l'Aigüeta 78** ☎ **972 64 24 85**

La Coloma

One of the best of La Bisbal's pottery shops. Everything is guaranteed hand-made. Striking designs and unusual earrings.

✉ **Carrer l'Aigüeta 75** ☎ **972 64 34 43**

Daró

Much of the pottery on sale here features bright colours and offbeat designs. There are also some beautiful Arab-style water-pots, which the locals fill with plants to adorn their courtyards and patios.

✉ **Carrer l'Aigüeta 76** ☎ **972 64 39 43**

L'Estació

Ming-style vases, homages to the Catalan design gurus such as Miró and Picasso, and ceramic cartoon characters for children can all be found among the casseroles and coffee pots in this eclectic pottery shop.

✉ **Carrer l'Aigüeta 18** ☎ **972 64 20 97**

Katy

Striking and imaginative pottery in colourful, child-like designs.

✉ **Carrer l'Aigüeta 41** ☎ **972 64 58 44**

Llensa

The big attraction of Llensa is the range of terracotta garden pots, including some antiques in a room at the back.

✉ **Carrer l'Aigüeta 91** ☎ **972 64 20 71**

Mediterrania

Here, there is a good selection of plain glazed terracotta plates, casseroles and urns.

✉ **Carrer l'Aigüeta 73** ☎ **972 64 17 00**

Nadal

A retail outlet boasting a big selection of pottery for the kitchen, home and garden.

✉ **Carrer l'Aigüeta 84** ☎ **972 64 03 88**

Rogenca d'Ullastret

Keep walking out of town beyond the other pottery shops and you will eventually come to this one, where everything is produced in a local workshop at Ullastret. The work here is strong on imaginative and individual designs.

✉ **Carrer l'Aigüeta 112**
☎ **972 64 04 82**

Vellí

Vellí is one of the biggest of La Bisbal's pottery shops. If you can't find what you are looking for here, you probably won't find it anywhere.

✉ **Carrer l'Aigüeta 60–68**
☎ **972 64 06 02**

Vila Clara

An arty pottery workshop where everything is designed and made locally – and surprisingly not as expensive as you might expect. Two shops, one at each end of town.

✉ **Carrer l'Aigüeta 56 and Carrer Sis d'Octubre 27** ☎ **972 64 25 79**

Olot
Regal i Art

A good place to find a wide range of innovative modern art created by the up and coming generation of Olot artists.

✉ **Plaça del Mig 202** ☎ **972 27 22 47**

Palafrugell
Plats i Olles

An interesting shop displaying a good range of locally produced artefacts and gifts, mostly in ceramics and glass.

✉ **Carrer Cavallers 33** ☎ **972 30 01 47**

Pals
Maria Puig de Buxó

This shop in the village centre sells a good range of pottery at competitive prices.

✉ **Carrer de la Creu 1** ☎ **972 63 68 41**

Peratallada
Les Voltes

Glass and pottery. Beneath the arches in the square.

✉ **Plaça de les Voltes** ☎ **972 63 41 21**

Torroella de Montgrí
Embolic

You can watch the beautiful tapestries being woven at this workshop close to the old town walls.

✉ **Avinguda Lluís Companys 22** ☎ **972 75 85 71**

Ullastret
Rogenca d'Ullastret

A practical workshop producing innovative ceramic designs.

✉ **Carrer Hospital 2** ☎ **972 75 76 65**

The North Coast & Beyond

Cadaqués
Arte Sacro

One of many little art galleries in the back streets of Cadaqués. This one specialises in religious art 'in memory of Salvador Dalí'.

✉ **Carrer Curós 18**

Figueres
Llibrería Surrealista

Dalí posters, prints, postcards and T-shirts, plus contemporary painting and jewellery – much more interesting than the official Dalí museum gift shop.

✉ **Plaça de Gala i Salvador Dalí** ☎ **972 50 70 70**

Shopping in Girona

The streets between the Rambla and the Jewish quarter are full of small, arty boutiques and galleries, specialising in everything from ceramics to candles. Some of the most interesting shops are on Carrer de les Ballesteries. Try Anna Casals for jewellery, La Carpa for masks and dolls, Ulysus for travel books, Eco-Opció for ethnic clothes and Dolors Turró for religious art.

Facilities &
Attractions

Looking after Children

Small children are particularly vulnerable to the sun and need to be well protected. Apply a high-factor sun block regularly, especially after swimming, and keep their heads covered during the heat of the day. If you hire a car, make sure that it has a child seat – book this in advance and check it carefully on arrival. The same goes for cots and high-chairs in hotels and apartments.

Facilities

The Costa Brava is an ideal destination for a holiday with children. Many hotels have nurseries and baby-sitting services, and package-tour operators lay on 'kids' clubs', with a wealth of activities to keep children amused. Every large resort has a children's playground and a mini-golf course, and probably a go-kart circuit and pony rides as well.

Most children are happy enough just playing on the beach – and the Costa Brava's beaches are perfect, with safe, shallow water, lots of sand and Red Cross posts in case of emergency. You can buy beach toys in all the resorts and hire out pedaloes on most of the beaches. For a bigger thrill, rent a child-size windsurfing board or take your kids for a boat trip around the coast. Although swimming is generally safe, the larger beaches operate a flag system and you should never let young children in or near the sea when the red or yellow warning flags are flying. The green flag means that it is safe to swim, but currents change quickly and you should still take care.

Children are often fascinated by new experiences of another culture, whether shopping in local markets, joining in with the *sardana* dance or coming across a noisy carnival parade. Wherever you go, you will find that your children are quickly making new friends. Like many other Spaniards, the Catalans love children and expect them to join in with whatever they do. It is quite normal to see children out at restaurants with their parents until midnight in summer, or playing on the beach while the adults finish off their liqueurs.

Attractions

The following is a selection of activities which will particularly appeal to children. Most of them only operate during the summer season, from May to October.

Amusement Parks

Magic Park

Funfair and indoor play area with roller-skating, a miniature boating lake, inflatable toys, dodgem cars, a carousel, video games and a soft play area for younger children. There is another Magic Park in Lloret de Mar.

✉ **Avinguda S'Agaró 86, Platja d'Aro** ☎ **972 81 78 64**
⏰ **Daily from 10AM**

Barcelona and the Costa Daurada

There is so much to see and do in Catalonia's thriving capital city that it falls outside the scope of this guide book. However, it is worth reminding visitors to the Costa Brava of the parts of Catalonia beyond Blanes, within easy reach even of the most northern resorts. The Costa Daurada is a coast of well-developed sandy beaches, stretching southwards to Barcelona. The city itself is an exciting place full of big city attractions. Among the highlights for children are the mountain-top funfair at Tibidabo, the world famous zoo and L'Aquarium, the largest in Europe.

Boat Trips

The Nautilus Adventure

See the world through a 'window in the bottom of the sea' Operating out of L'Estartit, the glass-hulled boats of this cruise company, one of several in this area, tours the Iles Medes Natural Park and the coast of the mainland.

✉ **Passeig Maritim 23, L'Estartit** ☎ **972 75 13 93** ⏰ **Daily, all year. Times may vary – call for details**

Museums

Museu Interactiu (Interactive Museum)

The sounds and sights of Pyrenean wildlife can be conjured up at the touch of a button at this interactive 'zoo'.

✉ **Carrer Dr Zamenhoff, Olot** ☎ **972 26 91 84** ⏰ **Daily 9–9**

Museu de Joguets

More than 3,000 traditional children's toys are on display in this charming toy museum. The exhibits include toy soliders, model trains and a teddy bear which once belonged to Salvador Dalí's sister. You can buy traditional wooden toys in the shop (➤ 62).

✉ **Carrer Sant Pere 1, Figueres** ☎ **972 50 45 85** ⏰ **Mon–Sat 10–1, 4–7, Sun 11–1:30**

Museu de la Nina (Doll Museum)

A collection of more than 300 dolls.

✉ **Plaça Lluís Companys, Castell d'Aro (near Platja d'Aro)** ☎ **972 81 71 79** ⏰ **Mon–Fri 5–9, Sat–Sun 11–1, 5–7 in summer; Sat–Sun 10–1, 5–8 in winter**

Water Parks

Aquadiver

If your children enjoy messing about in water, they'll love this – wave machines, zigzagging toboggans, safe white water rapids and a 'kamikaze' free-fall ride. Adults can relax too, with hydrotherapy and jacuzzis, and even very young children can have fun on the soft water slides and in the toddlers' adventure lake.

✉ **Carretera Circumval lació, Platja d'Aro** ☎ **972 81 88 68** ⏰ **Jun–Sep, daily from 10AM** 🚌 **Free bus from Platja d'Aro**

Marineland

Aquatic park with dolphin and sea lion shows and a small zoo with penguins and seals. There are also displays featuring parrots and birds of prey. Thrill rides include water chutes, toboggans, the Black Hole and the Canyon River ride (in a pneumatic tyre). There are separate pools and toboggan rides for the under-6s and a pleasant picnic area among the pine trees.

✉ **Carretera Malgrat a Palafolls, near Blanes** ☎ **937 65 48 02** ⏰ **Apr–Oct, daily 10–6**

Water World

Another great place for splashing about in the summer heat, with lots of pools, slides and the Water Mountain, where you can take a big-dipping roller-coaster ride in your own small boat.

✉ **Carretera Vidreres, Lloret de Mar** ⏰ **May–Oct, daily 10–6** ☎ **972 36 86 13** 🚌 **Free bus from Blanes, Lloret de Mar and Tossa de Mar**

Port Aventura

One of Europe's top theme parks is within reach of the Costa Brava, around two hours' drive south of Girona at Salou, near Tarragona. Port Aventura ☎ **977 77 90 90** is divided into five themed fantasy lands, each with thrilling rides and open-air shows. It is open 10–8 from mid-March to October and 10–midnight in July and August. Get there by taking the A7 motorway via Barcelona and leaving at exit 35.

Music & Art Festivals

The *Sardana*

Catalonia's national dance, in which men and women hold hands alternately around a circle, has been in existence for at least 500 years, but the modern form was invented in the 19th century. Banned under Franco, it has recently been revived and the circle is seen as representing the unity of the Catalan people. *Sardana* dances, accompanied by an 11-piece orchestra called a *cobla*, are often performed in village squares on Sundays and festival days, and anyone is welcome to join in.

Every summer the Costa Brava plays host to a number of music festivals, with concerts of classical, jazz and pop music taking place in monasteries, churches and castles. Some of the festivals, like those at Peralada and Torroella de Montgrí, attract internationally famous artists, like the Catalan opera singers Montserrat Caballé and José Carreras; others provide a platform for local musicians. For more information on music festivals, contact the local tourist office.

Central Costa Brava

Calella de Palafrugell

A festival of *havaneres* (➤ 43) is held on the beach on the first Saturday in July, and the Costa Brava jazz festival takes place in the gardens of Cap Roig throughout July and August. There are also festivals of *havaneres* in the neighbouring resorts of Llafranc (➤ 45) and Tamariu (➤ 52). Recitals of classical music take place throughout the year in the churches of Calella, Palafrugell and Llafranc and at the hilltop hermitage of Sant Sebastià between Llafranc and Tamarin.
☎ 972 30 02 28

Olot

The biggest *sardana* festival in Catalonia (see panel) takes place in Olot on the second or third Sunday of July, and features up to 5,000 dancers.
☎ 972 26 01 41

Torroella de Montgrí

The international music festival which takes place between July and August is one of the leading musical events in Europe, with performances ranging from chamber music to jazz in the town square and the Gothic church of Sant Genís.
☎ 972 76 06 05

The North Coast & Beyond

Cadaqués

An international festival of arts and music, both classical and contemporary, takes over this artists' village in August each summer.
☎ 972 25 83 15

Castelló d'Empúries

Music festival in the cathedral in August and a festival of minstrels, with traditional Catalan songs, on 11 September.
☎ 972 45 08 02

Figueres

A music festival takes place each August and September in the old monastery and church of Vilabertran.
☎ 972 50 31 55

Peralada

Top international performers appear each July and August in evening concerts in the grounds of the castle.
☎ 972 53 81 25

The South Coast & Beyond

Calonge

Concerts are held in the medieval castle each July.
☎ 972 66 17 14

Sant Feliu de Guíxols

One of the top festivals on the Costa Brava, with international musicians appearing at concerts in the parish church in July and August.
☎ 972 82 00 51

Nightlife

Bars and Clubs

Girona

Girona's club scene is particularly lively when the students are in town, between October and June. The busiest area is along Carrer Pedret, just north of the centre beside the River Ter.

Estrellat

Funk, rock and grunge music for a young and trendy crowd.

✉ **Carrer Lorenzana 49**
☎ **972 22 61 38** 🕐 **7PM–3AM**

Excalibur

'Celtic ale house' in the old town, where locals and visitors meet to drink British beers.

✉ **Plaça de l'Oli 1** ☎ **972 20 82 53**

Extreme de Nit

Late-night rock and pop on the outskirts of town. The Fashion's disco is next door.

✉ **Carrera Barcelona 179**
☎ **972 22 62 36** 🕐 **From 9PM Wed–Sat, 6PM Sun**

La Salsa

Cuban salsa and *merengue* music and rum cocktails.

✉ **Carrer Santiago 1** ☎ **972 21 47 27**

The North Coast
L'Hostal

Jazz club where Salvador Dalí famously spent an evening with Mick Jagger and Gabriel García Márquez, and still *the* in place to meet.

✉ **Passeig del Mar 8, Cadaqués** ☎ **972 25 80 00**
🕐 **12–4AM**

Casinos

Gambling was illegal in Spain during the Franco era, but the casinos are now operating again and there are two on the Costa Brava. Smart dress, including a jacket and tie for men is obligatory; you'll also need your passport to bet.

The North Coast
Casino Castell de Peralada

Tapestries line the walls of this moated Renaissance castle where you can play roulette, blackjack or *boule* in an atmosphere of elegance, luxury and fine dining.

✉ **Castell de Peralada** ☎ **972 53 81 25** 🕐 **Daily 7PM–4AM**

The South Coast
Casino de Lloret

This modern casino offers gaming machines, blackjack, roulette and Spanish card games, as well as a dinner-dance and cabaret each Saturday evening.

✉ **Carretera de Tossa, Lloret de Mar** ☎ **972 36 65 12**
🕐 **5PM–4AM**

Shows

Flamenco is a gypsy folk dance, with its origins in Andalusia, but it is popular all over Spain.

The North Coast
Patio

Flamenco and Spanish ballet with extravagant costumes and classical guitar music.

✉ **Carretera Roses-Figueres, Roses** ☎ **972 25 70 51**
🕐 **Nightly 9.30 in summer**

The South Coast
Gran Palace

Variety shows featuring flamenco and Spanish dancing. The shows are very popular with tour groups but it is possible to book individually.

✉ **Carretera Blanes, Lloret de Mar** ☎ **972 36 57 74**
🕐 **Nightly 8:45 in summer**

Discos

The mega-resorts of Lloret de Mar and Platja d'Aro are the nightlife hotspots of the Costa Brava. During the summer 'PR' people for the top discos tour the streets handing out free tickets to anyone deemed sufficiently young, sexy and hip. Disco fashions change with the seasons, but long-time favourites include Joy at Platja d'Aro and Tropics at Lloret de Mar. Most discos get busy around midnight and close at around 5AM.

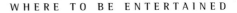

Sport

Bullfighting

The Catalans have always been more restrained than other Spaniards in their enthusiasm for bullfighting; ironically it is largely thanks to the tourist industry that it survives at all. The growing animal rights movement has succeeded in getting bullfights banned in Tossa de Mar, but they continue to take place in Lloret de Mar and Sant Feliu de Guíxols every Sunday in summer.

Golf

Clubs and trolleys are available for hire at all of the Costa Brava's seven golf courses. A reasonable standard of dress is expected.

Girona

Club de Golf Girona

Girona's golf course is situated in the northern suburbs.

✉ **Urbanització Golf Girona, Sant Julià de Ramis** ☎ **972 17 16 41**

Pals

Club de Golf de Pals

Pleasantly situated amid pine woods. Hosted the Spanish Open in 1984. A difficult course to play when the *tramuntana* wind gets up.

✉ **Platja de Pals** ☎ **972 63 60 06**

Torroella de Montgrí

Empordà Golf Club

✉ **Carretera Palafrugell-Torroella** ☎ **972 76 04 50**

The North Coast & Beyond

Figueres

Torremirona Golf Club

✉ **Carretera N260, Navata** ☎ **972 55 37 37**

Peralada

Peralada Golf Club

✉ **Paraje La Garriga** ☎ **972 53 82 87**

The South Coast

Platja d'Aro

Club Golf d'Aro Mas Nou

Spectacular course between Platja d'Aro and Palamós.

✉ **Urbanització Mas Nou** ☎ **972 82 69 00**

Club de Golf Costa Brava

This is a short but testing course with lots of narrow fairways, a few kilometres inland from the resort. The golf course has a hotel attached.

✉ **Santa Cristina d'Aro** ☎ **972 83 71 50**

Football

The Catalans are passionate about football and rarely get more animated than when watching FC Barcelona on television. The Costa Brava has none of the country's big-name teams, but local matches between club sides from Girona, Figueres and Olot can still cause a great deal of excitement. Most matches are played on Sundays between September and April; details can be found on posters or in the local papers.

Horse-riding

The gentle countryside of the Costa Brava is ideal for excursions on horseback, and there are riding schools and clubs in all the main resorts, as well as in inland towns like Banyoles, Begur and Palafrugell. Few Spanish riders wear protective hats, so it is a good idea to take your own, if you have one. Many of the riding clubs offer tuition for beginners, as well as pony rides for smaller children.

Tennis

There are good quality tennis courts at most of the main resorts, as well as at many of the hotels, apartment blocks and campsites along the coast. Enquire at tourist offices for details of local facilities.

Watersports

The calm waters and mild climate of the Catalan coast make it ideal for watersports, the only real hazard being the *tramuntana* wind from the north. Experienced sailors can explore the Costa Brava's many sheltered coves, while beginners can develop their skills at the larger beaches on the south coast.

Windsurfing, waterskiing, parascending and dinghy-sailing lessons are available at all the main resorts, as well as at Banyoles Lake, Spain's leading inland watersports location and scene of the rowing competitions during the 1992 Olympics in Barcelona. For a gentler, less energetic ride you can hire pedal boats, inflatables and canoes on all the main beaches. For advice on childrens's activities and beach safety ► 110.

Marinas

The Costa Brava is a popular stopping off point for yachting folk, sailing around the Mediterranean. The following marinas all have mooring and repair services available, though it is essential to book well ahead for facilities during the summer months. It is also possible to charter yachts at most of these ports or book short trips.

Aiguablava
62 moorings.
☎ 972 62 31 61

Blanes
320 moorings.
☎ 972 33 05 52

Cala Canyelles (Lloret de Mar)
130 moorings.
☎ 972 36 88 18

Colera
150 moorings.
☎ 972 38 90 95

Empúria-brava
4,000 moorings.
☎ 972 45 12 39

L'Escala
600 moorings.
☎ 972 77 00 16

L'Estartit
738 moorings.
☎ 972 75 14 02

Llafranc
140 moorings.
☎ 972 30 07 54

Llançà
500 moorings.
☎ 972 38 07 10

Palamós
867 moorings.
☎ 972 60 10 00

Platja d'Aro
862 moorings.
☎ 972 81 89 29

El Port de la Selva
328 moorings.
☎ 972 38 70 00

Portbou
104 moorings.
☎ 972 39 02 93

Roses
150 moorings.
☎ 972 25 70 03

Sant Feliu de Guíxols
260 moorings.
☎ 972 32 17 00

Santa Margarida (Roses)
1,100 moorings.
☎ 972 25 77 00

Scuba Diving
The clear waters of the Costa Brava make for excellent diving, especially around the Illes Medes near L'Estartit and the Illes Formigues between Palamós and Calella de Palafrugell. Diving schools in L'Estartit and Calella de Palafrugell can get you to the islands, and also offer one-day scuba-diving courses for beginners. All divers are required to take out insurance and are forbidden to fly for 24 hours after a dive.

What's On When

Carnival

The pre-Lenten carnival, with its riotous street parades and fancy dress balls, was banned under the Franco dictatorship, but has returned with a vengeance. Every town on the Costa Brava seems to organise its own carnival festivities, and the processions of floats at Platja d'Aro and Palamós, on the weekend before Shrove Tuesday, are some of the biggest in Spain. carnival ends with the 'burial of the sardine', signifying the end of winter.

January

Els Tres Reis (5–6 Jan): Children across Catalonia receive their Christmas presents when the Three Kings arrive in towns and villages by boat or on horseback.

February

Carnestoltes: pre-Lenten carnival parades (see panel).

March/April

Setmana Santa (Holy Week): on the evening of Maundy Thursday, men and boys dressed as skeletons march through Verges, near Torroella de Montgrí, performing a medieval 'dance of death'. Girona's Good Friday procession re-enacts Christ's death, with his crucified body carried to the cathedral by actors dressed as Roman soldiers. There is also a crucifixion ceremony on Good Friday in Sant Hilari Sacalm.
Festa de Sant Jordi (23 Apr): book and flower markets are set up in the streets in honour of Catalonia's patron, St George. The biggest festivities take place along the Rambla in Girona.

May

Carroussel Costa Brava (Whit Sunday): Palafrugell's Spring Festival was begun in 1963 to continue the carnival traditions following its prohibition. The highlight is the parade of floats on the Sunday afternoon.

June

Festa de Sant Joan (23–4 Jun): the eve of the feast of St John is marked with bonfires and firework parties all over Catalonia.

July

Cantada d'Havaneres (1st Sat): traditional sea-shanties on the beach at Calella de Palafrugell.
Aplec de la Sardana (2nd Sun): the biggest *sardana* festival takes place in Olot.
Mare de Déu del Carme (16 Jul): processions of fishing boats in the main ports in honour of the protector of fishermen.
Festa de Santa Cristina (24–6 Jul): Moorish dancing and a mass pilgrimage by boat from Lloret de Mar to the hermitage of Santa Cristina.

August

Fast painting contest (last Sun): in Tossa de Mar. The 'Mayor's Sardana' in Amer, between Girona and Vic, is an open, spiral dance, including everyone who wants to take part. It celebrates the unity between townspeople and dignitaries.

September

Festa del Tura (8 Sep): processions of giants, dwarves and hobby-horses in the streets of Olot.
La Diada (11 Sep): Catalonia's national day is marked all over the region by fireworks, street parades and *sardana* dancing.

October

Festa de Sant Narcís (late Oct): a fortnight of festivities in Girona, featuring bullfights, bonfires and parades of giants.

December

Nadal (Christmas, 24–5 Dec): midnight Mass is celebrated in churches across the region.

Practical Matters

Above: *in the Monday market at Torroella de Montgrí*
Below: *the signs are good in the Garrotxa Natural Park*

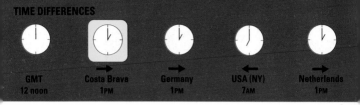

TIME DIFFERENCES

GMT 12 noon	Costa Brava 1PM →	Germany 1PM →	USA (NY) 7AM ←	Netherlands 1PM →

BEFORE YOU GO

WHAT YOU NEED

- ● Required
- ○ Suggested
- ▲ Not required

	UK	Germany	USA	Netherlands
Passport/National Identity Card	●	●	●	●
Visa	▲	▲	▲	▲
Onward or Return Ticket	▲	▲	●	▲
Health Inoculations	▲	▲	▲	▲
Health Documentation (Reciprocal Agreements ➤ 123)	●	●	▲	●
Travel Insurance	○	○	●	○
Driving Licence (National)	●	●	●	●
Car Insurance Certificate	●	●	●	●
Car Registration Document	●	●	●	●

WHEN TO GO

Costa Brava

High season

Low season

13°C	14°C	16°C	19°C	21°C	25°C	27°C	27°C	25°C	22°C	16°C	14°C
JAN	FEB	MAR	APR	MAY	JUN	JUL	AUG	SEP	OCT	NOV	DEC
🌧	☀️	🌦	🌦	🌦	☀️	☀️	☀️	🌦	🌦	🌧	🌧

🌧 Wet ☁️ Cloud ☀️ Sun 🌦 Sunshine & Showers

TOURIST OFFICES

In the UK
Spanish Tourist Office
22–3 Manchester Square
London W1M 5AP
☎ (020) 7486 8077;
Brochureline:
(0900) 166 9920)
Fax: (020) 7486 8034

In the USA
Tourist Office of Spain
666 Fifth Avenue (35th Floor)
New York
NY 10103
☎ (212) 265-8822
Fax: (212) 265-8864

Tourist Office of Spain
8383 Wilshire Boulevard
Suite 960
Beverley Hills
CA 90211
☎ (323) 658-7192
Fax: (323) 658-1061

POLICE (Policía Nacional/Mosso d'Esquadra) 091

FIRE (Bombers) 080

AMBULANCE (Ambulància) 061

IN ANY EMERGENCY YOU CAN RING 091 OR 112

WHEN YOU ARE THERE

ARRIVING

The main airport for the Costa Brava is Barcelona. The Spanish national airline, Iberia, has scheduled flights to Barcelona from major Spanish, other European and North American cities. In summer there are charter flights to Girona airport from cities in northern Europe.

Barcelona (El Prat) Airport Journey times
Kilometres to Girona

🚆	90 minutes
🚌	N/A
🚗	1 hour

100 kilometres

Girona-Costa Brava Airport Journey times
Kilometres to Girona

🚆	N/A
🚌	N/A
🚗	20 minutes

11 kilometres

MONEY

Spain's currency is the peseta, issued in notes of 1,000, 2,000, 5,000 and 10,000 pesetas and coins of 5, 10, 25, 50, 100, 200 and 500 pesetas. A one-peseta coin still exists but most bills are rounded down to the nearest 5 pesetas. Travellers' cheques are widely accepted in lieu of cash. On 1st January 1999 the euro became the official currency of Spain and the peseta became a denomination of the euro. Peseta notes and coins continue to be legal tender during a transitional period. Euro bank notes and coins are likely to be introduced by 1st January 2002.

TIME

Like the rest of Spain, Catalonia is one hour ahead of Greenwich Mean Time (GMT+1), except from late March to late October, when summer time (GMT+2) operates.

CUSTOMS

**YES
From another EU country for personal use (guidelines)**
800 cigarettes, 200 cigars, 1 kilogram of tobacco
10 litres of spirits (over 22%)
20 litres of aperitifs
90 litres of wine, of which 60 litres can be sparkling wine
110 litres of beer

From a non-EU country for your personal use, the allowances are:
200 cigarettes OR
50 cigars OR
250 grams of tobacco
1 litre of spirits (over 22%)
2 litres of intermediary products (eg sherry) and sparkling wine
2 litres of still wine
50 grams of perfume
0.25 litres of eau de toilette

The value limit for goods is 175 euros

Travellers under 17 years of age are not entitled to the tobacco and alcohol allowances.

**NO
Drugs, firearms, ammunition, offensive weapons, obscene material, unlicensed animals.

UK
93 366 62 00

Germany
93 292 10 00

USA
093 280 22 27

Netherlands
93 410 62 10

WHEN YOU ARE THERE

TOURIST OFFICES

- Blanes
  Plaça Catalunya
  ☎ 972 33 03 48

- Figueres
  Plaça del Sol
  ☎ 972 50 31 55

- Girona
  Rambla de la Llibertat 1
  ☎ 972 22 65 75

- Lloret de Mar
  Plaça de la Vila 1
  ☎ 972 36 47 35

- Olot
  Carrer Bisbe Lorenzana 15
  ☎ 972 26 01 41

- Palafrugell
  Carrer del Carrilet 2
  ☎ 972 30 02 28

- Tossa de Mar
  Avinguda del Pelegrí 25
  ☎ 972 34 01 08

- Vic
  Carrer Cintat 4
  ☎ 938 86 20 91

The above offices are open throughout the year. Most towns and villages have offices open in summer; look out for the international 🛈 sign.

The staff are usually multilingual and helpful and can supply you with local maps and guides.

NATIONAL HOLIDAYS

J	F	M	A	M	J	J	A	S	O	N	D
2		(1)	(1)	1	1		1	1	1	1	4

1 Jan	New Year's Day
6 Jan	Epiphany
Mar/Apr	Good Friday, Easter Monday
1 May	Labour Day
24 Jun	St John's Day
15 Aug	Assumption of the Virgin
11 Sep	Catalan National Day
12 Oct	Spanish National Day
1 Nov	All Saints' Day
6 Dec	Constitution Day
8 Dec	Feast of the Immaculate Conception
25 Dec	Christmas Day
26 Dec	St Stephens Day

Most shops, banks and offices close on these days but many places stay open in the main resorts.

OPENING HOURS

○ Shops		● Main post offices
● Offices		○ Museums
● Banks		○ Pharmacies

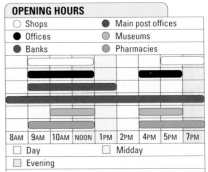

| 8AM | 9AM | 10AM | NOON | 1PM | 2PM | 4PM | 5PM | 7PM |

☐ Day ☐ Midday
☐ Evening

Most shops close on Saturday evening and all day on Sunday, though supermarkets and shops in the larger resorts may be open throughout the day seven days a week. Banks open Saturday mornings in the winter only. There will always be one pharmacist on duty in the main towns and the details will be published in local papers and shop windows.
Individual museum opening hours are listed throughout the guide. Many museums close on Mondays, and most vary their opening hours between summer and winter.

DRIVE ON THE RIGHT

TOILETS FREE

PUBLIC TRANSPORT

Internal flights Internal flights link Barcelona with other Spanish resorts, Madrid, Lisbon and the Balearic Islands.

Trains The main line from Barcelona to France passes through the Costa Brava region, with regular stops at Girona, Figueres and Portbou. There is also a branch line linking Barcelona and Girona with Blanes. For information on train services, call RENFE at Girona station ☎ 934 90 02 02.

Buses A wide network of local bus routes, operated by a number of private companies, the largest being Sarfa, connects Girona and Figueres with the main towns and villages of the Costa Brava. Extra routes connect the coastal resorts in summer. Timetables change, so check with your local tourist office or at the nearest bus station.

Boats A regular boat service in summer connects the resorts between Blanes and Palamós, with some boats continuing north as far as Tamariu. There are also various local services from the resorts of Cadaqués, Roses, Empúria-brava and L'Estartit. Details can be found on notices at the quayside in all the main resorts.

Urban Transport Although Barcelona has a well-developed urban transport network, the towns of the Costa Brava rely on buses and the national train network to connect them.

CAR RENTAL

The leading international car rental companies have offices at Barcelona and Girona airports. There are local car hire companies in the resorts. Keep the hire documents, your driving licence and your passport with you at all times.

TAXIS

Taxis can be hired at ranks or by flagging down a taxi with a green light on the roof. Prices are good, but there are supplements for late night, weekend and public holiday travel as well as for luggage and long-distance journeys, so check in advance.

DRIVING

Speed limit on motorways (*autopistas* – toll payable): **120kph**

Speed limit on main roads: **100kph** (minor roads **90kph**)

Speed limit on urban roads: **60kph**

Seat belts must be worn in front seats at all times and in rear seats where fitted.

Random breath-testing is carried out. The limit of 80 micrograms of alcohol per 100ml is strictly enforced.

Fuel (*gasolina*) is sold in various grades, including unleaded (*sense plomb*) and super-unleaded and diesel (*gasoil*). A few petrol stations are self-service but most have an attendant. Credit cards are widely accepted and at some you can pay at the pump using your card.

If you are driving your own car in Spain it is a good idea to take out European breakdown cover before you leave. Members of AIT-affiliated motoring clubs, including the AA, can use the services of the Real Automóvil Club de España (RACE ☎ 91 593 3333). Car-hire firms provide their own rescue service.

PERSONAL SAFETY

In an emergency, ask for the nearest police station (*comissaria*) and speak to the Policía Nacional, known in Catalonia as the Mossos d'Esquadra. Take sensible precautions to avoid crime:
• Don't carry more cash than you need.
• Never leave valuables on the beach or by the pool.
• Always lock your car with any valuables out of sight in the boot.
• Beware of pickpockets in crowded markets or tourist sights.

Police assistance:
☎ **091**
from any call box

TELEPHONES

Public telephones take 25-, 100- and 500 pta coins as well as phonecards (*teletarjetas*) which can be bought at post offices or tobacconists for 1,000 or 2,000 ptas. The cheap rate for international calls is weekdays 10PM–8AM, after 2PM Sat and all day Sun. For general information ☎ 1003; international telephone information: 025.

International Dialling Codes

From Spain to	
UK:	00 44
Germany:	00 49
USA & Canada:	00 1
Netherlands:	00 31

POST

Post offices (*Correus–Telègrafs*) in the main towns are open Mon–Sun 8–8, but in smaller towns Mon–Fri 9–1, 4–6, Sat 9–1 or open in the mornings only. Stamps (*segells*) can also be bought at kiosks and at *estancs* (tobacconists' shops). The main post office is in Girona ☎ 972 20 16 87

ELECTRICITY

The power supply in Spain is 220–225 volts. Sockets accept two-round-pin style plugs. Visitors from the UK require an adaptor and US visitors a transformer for appliances operating on 100–120 volts.

TIPS/GRATUITIES

Yes ✓ No ✗		
Restaurant	✓	10%
Cafés/bar	✓	change
Taxis	✓	10%
Tour guides	✓	100 ptas
Hairdressers	✓	100 ptas
Chambermaids	✓	100 ptas
Porters	✓	100 ptas
Cloakroom attendants	✓	change
Toilets	✗	

📷 **What to photograph**: rocky coastline, wild flowers, Romanesque churches, the old towns of Girona and Tossa de Mar.
Best time to photograph: early morning and evening, when the sunlight is subtle rather than overpowering.
Where to buy film: film and camera batteries are widely available in pharmacies (*farmàcias*) and tourist shops.

HEALTH

✚ **Insurance**
Citizens of European Union countries are entitled to free reciprocal health care in Spain on production of the relevant form (E111 in the UK). Private medical insurance is still advisable for emergencies, and essential for all non-European Union visitors.

Dental Services
Dental treatment is rarely covered by reciprocal health care agreements as most dentists only practise privately. Emergency dental treatment should be covered by private medical insurance.

☀ **Sun Advice**
Visitors from non-Mediterranean climates can burn quickly in the summer sun. It is best to avoid the midday sun altogether and to use a high-factor sun block, especially at first. Children are particularly vulnerable to the sun and should always wear a hat.

Drugs
Prescription and non-prescription drugs are available from pharmacies (*farmàcias*), distinguished by a large green cross. Recreational drugs, which you may be offered at nightclubs in the larger resorts, are illegal and should be avoided.

Safe Water
Tap water is generally safe to drink, but mineral water is cheap and easy to buy, either sparkling (*amb gas*) or still (*sense gas*). Remember, drink plenty of water to avoid dehydration.

CONCESSIONS

Students/Youths Holders of an International Student Identity Card (ISIC) may be able to obtain some concessions on travel and entrance fees. Anyone under 26 or belonging to a national youth hostel organisation can stay cheaply at the hostels (*albergues de joventut*) in Girona, Figueres, Olot and Empúries.

Senior Citizens There are few specific discounts available for senior citizens, though it is always worth checking at museums and tourist attractions. A number of hotels and tour operators offer economical deals on long-stay winter holidays, when the savings in the cost of fuel bills can almost wipe out the cost of the trip.

CLOTHING SIZES

Spain	UK	Europe	
46	36	46	36
48	38	48	38
50	40	50	40
52	42	52	42
54	44	54	44
56	46	56	46 Suits
41	7	41	8
42	7.5	42	8.5
43	8.5	43	9.5
44	9.5	44	10.5
45	10.5	45	11.5
46	11	46	12 Shoes
37	14.5	37	14.5
38	15	38	15
39/40	15.5	39/40	15.5
41	16	41	16
42	16.5	42	16.5
43	17	43	17 Shirts
36	8	34	6
38	10	36	8
40	12	38	10
42	14	40	12
44	16	42	14
46	18	44	16 Dresses
38	4.5	38	6
38	5	38	6.5
39	5.5	39	7
39	6	39	7.5
40	6.5	40	8
41	7	41	8.5 Shoes

WHEN DEPARTING

- Remember to contact the airport or your tour operator on the day before leaving to confirm flight details.
- Arrive at the airport at least two hours before your flight, leaving time to return your hire car if necessary.
- The duty-free shops at Barcelona airport sell a wide range of alcohol, tobacco, gifts, perfume, fashions, jewellery, music and toys.

LANGUAGE

Since 1979 Catalan (*Català*) has returned to being the official language of Catalonia, and although Spanish is still universally understood, it is Catalan that you are most likely to see and hear on the streets. A Romance language, with its roots in ancient Latin, it is spoken in Valencia, Andorra, the Balearic islands and parts of the French Pyrenees, as well as in Catalonia. Many Catalan words look like their equivalents in French or Spanish – but the sound of the language (definitely *not* a dialect of Spanish) is utterly distinct.

hotel	*hotel*	toilet	*vàter*
campsite	*càmping*	balcony	*balcó*
apartment	*apartament*	sea view	*vista al mar*
single room	*habitació senzilla*	one night	*una nit*
double room	*habitació doble*	breakfast	*esmorzar*
bath	*bany*	key	*clau*
shower	*dutxa*	lift	*ascensor*
washbasin	*lavabo*	stairs	*escala*

bank	*banc*	banknote	*bitllet de banc*
exchange bureau	*oficina de canvi*	credit card	*carta de crèdit*
		change	*canvi*
cashier	*caixer*	how much?	*quant és?*
travellers' cheque	*xec de viatge*	expensive	*car*
foreign currency	*moneda estrangera*	cheap	*bon preu*
		post office	*correus*
		stamp	*segell*

lunch	*dinar*	water	*aigua*
dinner	*sopar*	sparkling	*amb gas*
menu	*carta*	still	*sense gas*
set menu	*menú*	beer	*cervesa*
waiter	*cambrer*	draught beer	*una canya*
waitress	*cambrera*	dessert	*postre*
white wine	*vi blanc*	coffee	*cafè*
red wine	*vi negre*	the bill	*el compte*

airport	*aeroport*	taxi	*taxi*
aeroplane	*avió*	car	*cotxe*
station	*estació*	garage	*garatge*
train	*tren*	petrol station	*gasolinera*
bus	*autobús*	petrol	*gasolina*
boat	*vaixell*	unleaded	*sense plomb*
ticket	*bitllet*	motorway	*autopista*
return	*anar i tornar*	bicycle	*bicicleta*

yes	*sí*	sorry	*ho sento*
no	*no*	welcome	*benvinguts*
please	*sisplau*	open	*obert*
thank you	*gràcies*	closed	*tancat*
hello	*hola*	do you speak English?	*parla anglès?*
good morning	*bon dia*		
good afternoon	*bona tarda*	I don't speak Catalan	*no parlo català*
goodnight	*bona nit*		
goodbye	*adéu*	I don't understand	*no ho entenc*
excuse me	*perdoni*		

Acknowledgements

The Automobile Association would like to thank the AA in Ireland, and the following photographers, libraries, associations and individuals for their assistance in the preparation of this book.

MARY EVANS PICTURE LIBRARY 10b; ROBERT HARDING PICTURE LIBRARY 35b, 88, 89b; HULTON GETTY 11a, 11b, 14b; INTERNATIONAL PHOTOBANK F/Cover d (Flamenco dancer); MOSSOS D'ESQUADRA, GIRONA 122b; MRI BANKERS' GUIDE TO FOREIGN CURRENCY 119; PICTURES COLOUR LIBRARY 8c, 9b, 20b; REX FEATURES LTD 14c; SALVADOR DALÍ/FOUNDATION GALA-SALVADOR DALÍ/DACS 60; SPECTRUM COLOUR LIBRARY 27b, 57b; WORLD PICTURES 31a, 76b, 80b;

All remaining pictures are held in the Association's library (AA PHOTO LIBRARY) and were taken by Michelle Chaplow with the exception of the following pages:
P Baker 9c; T Boyer 12c; S L Day 56b; J Edmanson B/Cover, 13b, 73a; P Enticknap 16b, 87; J A Tims 59, 60a, 61a, 62a, 63a, 65a, 68a, 69a, 70a, 71a, 72a; P Wilson 1

The photographer would like to thank Partonato de Girona for their assistance.

Copy editor: Nia Williams **Paste-up:** Stuart Perry
Revision management: Outcrop Publishing Services, Cumbria

Dear Essential Traveller

Your comments, opinions and recommendations are very important to us. So please help us to improve our travel guides by taking a few minutes to complete this simple questionnaire.

You do not need a stamp (unless posted outside the UK). If you do not want to cut this page from your guide, then photocopy it or write your answers on a plain sheet of paper.

Send to: **The Editor, AA World Travel Guides, FREEPOST SCE 4598, Basingstoke RG21 4GY.**

Your recommendations…

We always encourage readers' recommendations for restaurants, nightlife or shopping – if your recommendation is used in the next edition of the guide, we will send you a *FREE* AA *Essential* Guide of your choice. Please state below the establishment name, location and your reasons for recommending it.

_____

_____

_____

_____

Please send me **AA *Essential*** _____

(*see list of titles inside the front cover*)

About this guide…

Which title did you buy?

AA *Essential* _____

Where did you buy it? _____

When? m m / y y

Why did you choose an AA *Essential* Guide? _____

_____

_____

_____

_____

Did this guide meet your expectations?

Exceeded ☐   Met all ☐   Met most ☐   Fell below ☐

Please give your reasons _____

_____

_____

_____

continued on next page…

Were there any aspects of this guide that you particularly liked? _____

_____

_____

_____

Is there anything we could have done better? _____

_____

_____

_____

_____

About you…

Name (*Mr/Mrs/Ms*) _____

    Address _____

_____

_____ Postcode _____

    Daytime tel nos _____

Which age group are you in?
Under 25 ☐   25–34 ☐   35–44 ☐   45–54 ☐   55–64 ☐   65+ ☐

How many trips do you make a year?
Less than one ☐   One ☐   Two ☐   Three or more ☐

Are you an AA member? Yes ☐   No ☐

About your trip…

When did you book? m m / y y   When did you travel? m m / y y
How long did you stay? _____
Was it for business or leisure? _____
Did you buy any other travel guides for your trip?
    If yes, which ones? _____

_____

Thank you for taking the time to complete this questionnaire. Please send
it to us as soon as possible, and remember, you do not need a stamp
(*unless posted outside the UK*).

Happy Holidays!